Eternal Life

The Mended Loom

Steve Cox

Onwards and Upwards Publishers

3 Radfords Turf, Cranbrook, Exeter, EX5 7DX, United Kingdom

www.onwardsandupwards.org

This first edition published in the United Kingdom by Onwards and Upwards Publishers (2017).

ISBN: 978-1-911086-92-5
Typeface: Sabon LT
Editor: Sharon Fletcher
Illustrations: Leah-Maarit
Graphic design: LM Graphic Design

Printed in the United Kingdom.

About the Author

 Steve is a retired GP living in Shropshire. He is married to Caroline, and they run a holiday cottage for peace, quiet and reflection. Steve has always loved Christian discussion, and science. He also enjoys playing in the river in the garden, and playing the piano. His parents were missionaries, and Steve was brought up in East Africa, mostly in remote areas.

To contact the author, please write to

stephencox267@gmail.com

You can also read his blog at

roughgrounds.wordpress.com

or scan the QR barcode below with your smartphone:

Eternal Life

Contents

Eternal Life

Preface

A recurring theme in life as a church member is the difficulty experienced when considering suffering in the context of a good God. This, combined with the changing interface of the church with modern culture has generated many discussions which often end inconclusively. The response of reformed Christians to these challenges often gravitates towards the inadequacy of human understanding when dealing with an eternal God. Uncertainty is often painful and requires the practice of faith.

After a series of home-group meetings where it became clear that there is widespread disquiet with the evangelical position, I decided to actually find out what aspects of (much maligned) Calvinism really hold true, and why. At the same time, I had a renewed interest in the idea of the kingdom of heaven as the present dwelling place for anyone who calls themself Christian. This was associated with a strong sense of the centrality of the resurrection (as a defining belief); I felt as if I had been asleep for several years; here was a reminder of the excitement with which my faith had started when I began this journey!

While these two subjects were at the top of my thoughts (the eternal God and the risen Lord Jesus), I found myself looking at human structure and the definition of a life. This might be considered natural while rounding off a medical career where the actions of nurture and nature are so often intricately interwoven to produce the good and bad results that appear in the consulting room. My grandfather, the statistician Ronald Fisher, had famously within family folklore made comments (if not performed actual experiments!) on the actions of genes and environment in his children. It was thus unsurprising that I should be delighted to stumble across an illustration of the inter-relations between nurture and nature in the weaving of cloth.

This book is the result of considering the eternal nature of God, the resurrection of Christ and the effects of this on the structure of man. Once the initial illustration has been drawn, I have used it, I hope consistently, to bind the rest of the book together. The book thus falls into three parts:

1. Resurrection and the Fall (with an illustration of human structure).
2. A tangle with TULIPs (Calvinist doctrines!)
3. Specific areas of doctrine that challenge Christians nowadays.

Introduction

Time and space are commonplace subjects. We use them, observe them and talk about them regularly, but we seldom progress in their comprehension. One other subject of universal concern is death. It is part of every human life, but its doorway leads into the complete unknown. We hear about it and sometimes see it happening, but when it comes to considering ourselves experiencing it, death is utterly beyond analysis. These three areas are therefore mysteries. Physicists study and attempt to describe time and space. The other side of the door to death, insofar as it might impinge on our existence, seems to be the province of dreamers, fantasists, spiritualists – and theologians. In this book, I will be looking at death from the standpoint of Christian theology.

Time and space are also hard to grasp because we are creatures who live 'inside' them. I think it is generally agreed that the human mind cannot comprehend or encompass time and space without tools to aid it. Mathematics has been the tool which we have found that we need if we are to visualise time and space in any way beyond simple experience. Mathematics may have its own existence or it may not, but physicists use it continuously when describing time and space.

It is also very difficult to look at death objectively! We might gain more understanding about death – as we have not got an external vantage point – by using comparisons and visualisations. It is often easier to comprehend a difficult subject using pictures taken from a different context.

In this book, I have used illustrations from the physical world with the intention of clarifying some points about death and our lives in the context of eternity.

As I have written, I have looked at 'the life of a human' as a concept in many of the chapters. I hope it is clear that I am not using the word 'life' simply in a biological context. Biologists must forgive me for redefining 'life' to include our own sense of self and awareness – our soul, if you will. This may have little scientific meaning, but it does have a personal meaning to every reader of this book. Like time, space and death, it is quite impossible at present to put our life onto a microscope slide. Even if a unified physical theory of everything hits the journals, an explanation for life will not be included in it. Life in this sense seems to obstinately remain a mystery. If we do not have a detailed understanding of life, then a scientific comprehension of death is certain to elude our grasp!

In this book, I am describing areas not covered by scientific theory. In the past, it has been tempting to identify the mysteries of science with the mysteries of God. This view has long been abandoned by theologians and faith groups. During the enlightenment period, this policy always ended up with a 'God of the gaps' – steadily being eroded by scientists who expected to understand all things in the near future and thus render God redundant. Periodically, news was broadcast that this or that discovery had "rendered God dead". These discoveries have without fail resulted in subsequent realisation that "reports of my demise were greatly exaggerated". I can report that the situation regarding God's death remains an area where the subjective judgement of the person far outweighs any objective ruling by 'science'.

The situation now is actually very different (and far more interesting!) Fewer and fewer scientists believe in the enlightenment view that all things can be comprehensible to man. As an indication of this, I think it is legitimate to note that mathematics itself has been unable to find its own axiomatic roots. It is generally accepted now that there are some areas where it is 'impossible to know'. It might seem that God can again take up his hiding place in the incomprehensible! To rely on this would be a great mistake, however. I have always believed that God is not confined simply to those areas at present unknown to us. The God who manifests in mystery has also manifested through Creation. If this is the case, then the unknowable gaps are no more important than the things which we see and feel and understand well. We experience life every day and Creation surrounds us and fills our senses. In this book, I am writing about a Deity who walks easily in our daily experience as well as in the "numinous" (to quote C.S. Lewis[1]) and also the absolutely incomprehensible. To follow the footsteps of

---

[1] C.S. Lewis; *The Problem of Pain.*

that Deity into the unknown I have taken the liberty of using some pictures taken from the language of science. I have also used ordinary pictures from everyday life. I hope these clarify rather than complicate.

Can any book bring any better understanding of the unknowable? If Gödel, Hilbert and their predecessors reached an exhausted halt, then this study of life (in the context of death, time, space and the regions surrounding them) is obviously doomed to run out of steam well before that; I am nevertheless building my bridge more from the theological and faith side of the chasm, using some illustrations from the scientific side, so I hope to shine a dim light on some aspects of these mysteries that are not often considered. It is surprising to me that in doing so, my thoughts have crossed some fairly well-trodden highways of theology and science.

I have started the discussion fairly abruptly with definitions; I hope that this does not prove too startling. Having considered life and the Fall, I have (like an urban base-jumper) launched my thesis from a platform that I have no rights to enter, or experience of starting from – eternity.

From this initial discussion, I have gaily jumped into a section trying to square the circle of Calvinism and Arminianism regarding destiny.

Naturally, having bounced around this serious topic like an errant puppy disturbing the Lord Mayor's parade, I have begun to appreciate 'doubt' as a concept, and thus continued into a consideration of uncertainty in various aspects of life. I have ended with a reflection about joy, which I hope will divert attention from the manifest errors in understanding and expression that the reader may be smarting from (if indeed they have survived reading the book that far).

You have my best wishes if you wish to proceed further.

CHAPTER ONE

What Is Resurrection?

Resurrection is the renewal of life despite death. Life is the life of the soul, not just of the body or brain; it is the ideal, essence or heart of the person. It is the spirit. It is the real person, the hand inside the puppet. In human terms, it is the ability to stand outside ourselves and be aware of our own self as separate from all others. It is the "Who am I?" and the answer – "It is me." Awareness of these things is seated largely in the brain in our bodies. Human life in its development to mature form has memory enough to give the person a trajectory. That trajectory is unique, and is part of a life's journey that exceeds its birth, as a rocket's flight exceeds its launch pad.

In existential terms, the life of a person is an event in eternity, and the event is one event, with no partition of that event. By this I mean that when we talk about a person in relation to resurrection we must consider every part of that person's life, including the future person, if that person is still alive. We tend to look at resurrection as if it were a single event which we 'look forward to'. It will be helpful while reading this book to look at our life as if it were a fish being caught. If we see resurrection as an event 'in the future', that is like seeing the fish caught by a fishing line which pulls the fish out of the water from just one end.

Figure 1. Pulling a fish out from one end.

In this illustration, this represents us being 'raised from the dead' at the end of our life (obviously, the older end!) I am suggesting that it is better to visualise resurrection by thinking of a fishing net, which pulls the whole fish out from all sides and both ends!

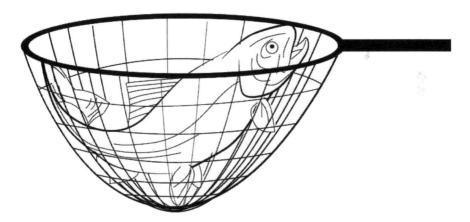

Figure 2. Taking the whole fish from all sides.

This means that we are not seeing resurrection as an event in a linear timeline (which is how we normally see things), but we are seeing resurrection acting on all our times at once. We thus include our life as a whole in our resurrection, which may be quite alien to normal thought for many of us.

It might be helpful in visualising this to introduce a concept from a physicist's representation of the universe. I have found this picture useful in comprehending a 'whole life'. To a physicist, the smallest part of a beam of light is both a wave and a particle (a photon). This particle travels at the fastest velocity that is possible. At the speed of light, it is accepted that 'time stands still' for the particle. It is therefore acceptable (although not easy) to think of a beam of light as leaving a star and arriving at our eyeball at exactly the same instant (for the particle).

Figure 3. An instant journey.

Although this is almost incredible, it is not the point I wish to make. The more amazing aspect to me is that the passage of that light beam across space in an instant (from its own perspective!) is a physical link between the object emitting that beam and the object receiving the beam. In a physicist's language, it is a quantum event. The quantum event in this example might be described in more detail thus: as an electron in the star dropping down to a lower energy level, emitting that energy in the light beam, and sending it directly to another electron in the retinal cell (the rod) in the eye of the beholder, which absorbs that energy and jumps to a higher energy level. Almost unbelievably, no matter how far away the origin of the photon is from the destination (and thus 'in the past' from the destination), there is a real sense in which the source and destination communicate by 'aligning' advanced and retarded waves in an 'atemporal' way. This implies that the source (say two hundred years ago in a star two hundred light years away) only releases the quantum of energy (carried in the photon) when a suitable destination electron (maybe in the eye of an observer) is available to receive it. How the source 'finds' the (two hundred years in the future) destination is said to be achieved 'atemporally'.[2]

That whole process is tied up into a bundle called a quantum event. It is remarkable that a quantum event is a single thing. It is not possible to untie it and dissect it into the parts I have described above. That description is a pleasing story I have told you to help you visualise a quantum event, but please do not think of the story as the whole truth! It is a mental picture.

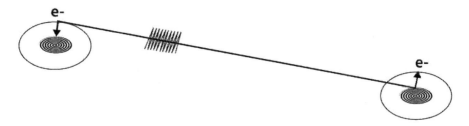

Figure 4. A quantum event.

If you have followed this explanation, I will now apply it to 'a life'. In this picture, our conception is the origin of the event of our life, as the electron is the origin of the photon. The trajectory and termination of our lives are, like the path and destination of the photon, also part of that event, and exist with no division from the origin of that event. It is as if our whole life, looked at from an eternal perspective (that is, one outside time), can be considered as a single thing. If this seems unlikely, then you are in my backyard (!), but both you and I must accept that quantum events happen all the time, and respectable, suited scientists are able to live their lives seeing stars that are millions of miles away, knowing all the time that when they look at them, the particles of light arriving at their eyes are no older than when they left the stars (despite hundreds of years passing in the ordinary world around them). They are able to live with the commonplace knowledge that the quantum events described above occur both in those stars billions of miles away and in

[2] Gilbert. N. Lewis; PROC. N. A. S. PHYSICS VOL. 12, 1926.
John G. Cramer; 28 Feb 2015; arXiv:1503.00039 Cornell university library.

their own eyes *and (for the particle) at the same time and being the same event!*

I will now return to looking at 'a life'. How can this picture help us to understand resurrection?

Many millions of people believe in eternal life. This theological concept is commonly taken to mean the continued existence of the person in time beyond the one guaranteed event in every life, which is death. This has given rise to many concepts and traditions, including those we have of ghosts (who represent the continued, if insubstantial relic of the living person after they have died). When I mentioned resurrection in the second paragraph of this chapter, I noted that normally we think of resurrection as another event on our timeline, occurring after we die. The picture that I have introduced, that of a single united life – from birth to death – one undivided thing, implies that we might look for resurrection elsewhere. This might help us to reconsider our traditional thoughts of ghosts and spirits. It might also help when we have problems considering where people reside after death and prior to 'rising again'. I will try to unfold this concept in a further illustration.

If we see our life including its time dimension as one entity (a four-dimensional object), we find that we automatically picture it within 'another space'. For convenience, I will call that space 'eternity'.

Our whole life, including its time dimension, exists in eternity, and although it stops (in the time dimension) at death, it does not cease. Resurrection is the process by which the life exists in eternity. To look at our life as if it ceases at death is the same as looking at a square from its edge and only seeing a line. The line defines a single dimension of the square, and appears to end at the corner of the square; however, behind the line there are infinitely many lines which are equally part of that square.

In this illustration, our completed life is seen as that square. The limitation of this space-time universe means that the whole life cannot be seen properly 'from here'! We are limited to seeing it sequentially unfolding, one moment after another. I hope that this picture allows us to accept that there might be a possibility of further (not necessarily future!) existence beyond the life of moments that we experience.

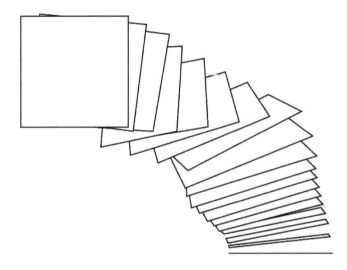

Figure 5. Seeing a square from the side.

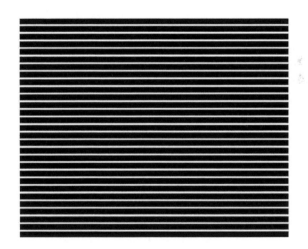

Figure 6. A square as an infinite number of lines.

To truly understand what resurrection is, it is helpful to look at the reason it is needed. That reason is commonly termed 'the Fall'. I will be looking at this in more detail in the next chapter, but at this point will briefly try to show why it necessitates resurrection.

The Fall (of man) caused a separation of our life from our eternal presence, and this limited us to live a life of moments which appear unconnected to our 'eternal self' (in the illustration above, one line might be part of a square, but gets sliced off). In this sense, every moment of our lives could be seen as separated from our whole selves. This could be seen as another sort of death. If we accept the validity of the illustration we might see that it is a daily death that we die. By this I mean that the 'line of our life' should really be in connection with the rest of the square at every point. On any day of our lives, we might expect some awareness of the rest of our existence. The fact that we have no such awareness might be a result of this separation. Our line of life would then culminate in the final death when our bodies decay. The Fall effectively partitions the event which should not be partitioned – our completed life. This then changes the meaning of 'completed life' from 'fulfilled life' to 'terminated life'.

This might help us appreciate the meaning of resurrection. In this picture, resurrection could be seen as the reconnection of our daily being with our actual fulfilled and eternal being. This eternal being is, or was, or will be filled with life, and the life is individual but connected to the source of all lives.

In order to understand human nature, the Fall and original sin, it is necessary to look at the change that the resurrection makes to our lives.

If we do not consider as central the reconnection of our life to eternal life, we may easily perceive an incomplete and thus confused picture of ourselves. This might be the basis of many misinterpretations of the nature of our Redemption, grace and, indeed, God's nature.

What then is the nature of the life we so often take for granted?

As stated above, we presently see or experience a life of moments, spread out through the calendar of our history. We have not got an eternal perspective, so, typically, we look at a daily waking up, reorientation into consciousness, a sequence of events, acts, thoughts and reactions, and then a subsidence into sleep.

Here we process the activity of the day into memories, and these form a system of backdrops (or sets, if a theatrical metaphor may be used), against which we play out the rest of our moments. Any assumption we might have that this perceived sequence of days is a contiguous whole must be dropped, despite appearances to the contrary.

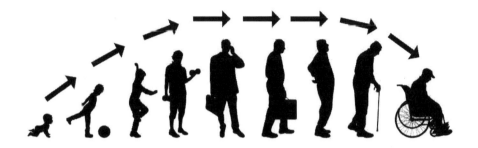

Figure 7. A lifetime.

We have lives that are like a Victorian zoetrope, with separated pictures all around the inside: start them rotating, lights on, apply eye to slit and, hey presto, a moving image.

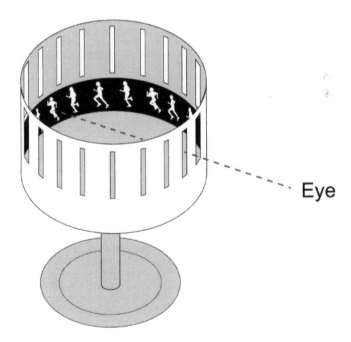

Figure 8. Zoetrope.

Our daily moments line up, and so long as we are not drunk, on drugs or otherwise impaired, we see a smooth sequence of memories telling us just who we think we are. It only takes a short excursion into sleep, however, to throw a few doubts into our self-conceived notion of identity. In the land of dreams, we find places that do not obey normal sense. Unreal, dreams may be, but real enough they seem at the time, and the same holds true with memories. I have termed this the 'life of moments', as a short phrase to imply the necessary biological structures and functions that compose our brains, and which are currently becoming better understood by scientists. How it is that our brains generate and contain our earthly selves is a wonderful and complex matter. I cannot tell you how it works, but would ask you to share my amazement at the current increase in knowledge of how the brain functions! It is noteworthy that Einstein himself may have had a concept of the life of separated moments.[3]

If we limit our selfhood to a biologically-observed machine, however complex, we end up with our humanity and individuality (the life that I defined at the start of the chapter and have described in the previous paragraph) being placed into a 'subjective trap'. What I mean by this is that our biological and psychological self fails to describe the full human experience. I have found that if I limit my selfhood to a biological or psychological description, most of the features which make me 'me' end up slipping away into a dreamlike notion that has little substance. We therefore have to be careful that our understanding of eternal life avoids confusion with a dream world or, indeed, a 'spiritual existence', lacking in the solidity of reality. I suspect (with some caution) that the problem of whether 'we ourselves' are simply a neurochemical froth of consciousness, or whether our own deep conviction of selfhood is based in an objective reality separate from that observable chemistry, may find its answer in the link with a timeless reality at present obscure to our senses, based as they are in our time and space.

---

[3] W. Sullivan; *The Einstein papers: a man of many parts;* New York Times, March 29, 1972. See Hadot 2011, 169; 205 n. 4.

We are all indebted to C.S. Lewis for his insistence that eternal life is objective and solid! In 'The Great Divorce'[4], the entrance lobby to heaven is portrayed as having far greater solidity than the ghostlike human souls who cluster there. This image (for it is only an image) helps us to understand that heaven is not a 'state of mind', but an external reality which exists independently from us. Einstein taught us that time and space exist interdependently with matter, the one causing the other, neither standing alone. In the Bible, John 1 teaches us that God spoke the Word which brought everything into being. This brings to mind a cartoon depicting the space-time continuum expanding all around us as nothing more than a speech-bubble proceeding from the mouth of God. As far as I can tell, this picture still gives as good a raison d'être as anything Stephen Hawking has managed 'around the back' of the Big Bang! It is impossible for any picture we draw to really exclude the time dimension from our presuppositions, however, so I will leave the cosmological picture right there. We remain subjective beings crawling across a web of days, so, how can we escape into eternal life?

Two keys to help unlock the prison of a time-based life

There is one commonly-held philosophy or religion that gives funda-mental importance to attempts to deal with existence after death. Please forgive me if I turn to it here. I hope that if you are of a different faith or of no faith, you might be gracious to me as I use the best tool I know of to come closer to understanding this issue. The first key that the Christian view of resurrection gives us to unlock this subjective trap is the statement in the biblical book of Colossians (chapter 1, verse 18) that Jesus Christ was the first to rise again. This lays down the axiom that Jesus became the first eternal man. The importance of this is that in this view there is at least one human who now stands outside the life of moments, having a continuous presence, not limited by biological or cosmological structure. If what Christians believe is true, the life of Jesus is in an eternal frame, thus he can encompass all the moments of

---

[4] C.S. Lewis; *The Great Divorce.* Many references, e.g. Chapter 4, paragraph 1.

all our lives. He, as it were, stands outside our normal timeframe, and sees "yesterday, today, forever", as the old song goes.

As Jesus has gone before, so we can also possibly accept that our own moments may all add up to something eternal; this is something that we can do from within our life of moments. This is what is meant by a step of faith – a determination to believe in the resurrection of Jesus. After this step has been taken, the reality of the existence of a 'joined-up life', existing in eternity, is something that proceeds from it.

I have to borrow an analogy[5] from C.S. Lewis to help here. How can an eternal life proceed from a temporal decision to believe in Jesus' resurrection? Lewis imagines a set of books which have existed forever, one on top of the other. In this situation, the position of the top book depends on the bottom book, but not because the bottom book came first. Lewis freely admits that he has substituted a spatial dependence for a temporal one, but the point is made. An eternal life can result 'from all eternity' from a temporal decision 'to believe on Christ'. Jesus is the key to this: whoever we are and whenever we live, his transit from death to life is the basis on which we ourselves can connect up to an eternal reality. He enables the process for the rest of us.

The second key that unlocks the prison of the 'days of our lives' has been mentioned above. It is the decision to believe in the resurrection. It has been said by G.K. Chesterton[6] that when something actually happens to us, it happens and then afterwards we notice it. This is an observation that we live at one step's remove from reality. We observe ourselves, and in that observation, we miss the actual experience. The decision to believe in the resurrection is like seeing a cake in a shop window and then realising that we are definitely going to go in and buy that cake. If we find ourselves debating whether it is the right thing to do, then the decision has not been made. In some ways, the decision to buy the cake 'makes us', rather than us making it.

I remember lying in bed at the age of nine or ten in boarding school worrying about life and death and bad things happening. All at once I remembered the promise "that by believing you may have life in his name". I could not have told you that this was from John 20:31, but

---

[5] C.S. Lewis; *Mere Christianity;* Chapter 4: The Good Infection, paragraph 2.
[6] G.K. Chesterton. *The Napoleon of Notting Hill.*

the meaning of the quote had penetrated my young brain! The decision was made almost before I had thought the thought. When I looked back on it, it seemed so simple that it was almost cheating! It was such a relief to hand over the worries, that you might say I was tempted into faith by my desire to avoid mental pain.

This is, of course, one argument of the faithless against faith. And yet, when it comes to the decision to believe, I reckon that it absorbs our whole mental being – and that includes our imagination, our desires, our fears, our pleasures and all of the things that make us into the individual that we are. There is automaticity about the decision – it is almost as if we suddenly realised a fact about ourselves, rather than that we made a mental decision. This is of course what we might expect if we look at a transition from a life of moments to an eternal presence. If our life is a sequence of forming moments, then we might make decisions considering all our past experiences and thus making a judgement. If, however, our life is an eternal event, then a major life decision may be more like a discovery of something that we already were![7] The reason that both these seemingly contradictory views of the decision are correct is bound up in the fact that we are composed of memories that are physical entities in our brains, but we are also an eternal being linked to those memories. We are a bit like an amphibian living in two worlds at once.

The decision to believe (the step of faith in the resurrection) is itself an eternal twist in our story; whether we see it as something that 'one did' or something that 'is a description of me' are simply perceptions from different sides of eternity. What matters is that the step of faith to believe the fact that Christ became alive again after death makes a link between us and that life. It means that the moments that we live are lived in the context of a life (his life!) which became more than a sequence of moments. This has profound consequences for the way we think, for the way we act, and for all our relationships. If death is not the concluding part of our lives, then our thoughts must of necessity become other thoughts. Our emotions must change. Our actions must change. Our morality must change. Our investments must change. Our relationship to possessions must change. It all seems overwhelming, but,

---

[7] See Appendix for relevant quotes attributed to Mozart, Boethius and Proclus.

in reality, it is automatic because the eternal link, once made, alters our decisions so that the changes become natural to us.

/

CHAPTER TWO

What Is the Fall of Man?

The Fall is the continuing event of separation of man from God, from our eternal existence. It is the cause of the fragmentation of an eternal person into a 'life of moments'. This life of separated moments gradually allows us to become people who are not what we would have hoped to be. We contradict ourselves by actions which do not cohere across our lives. We lose ourselves, we become confused and we struggle to determine our direction. We lose our peace – that peace which comes from knowing who we are and from being fully that person in all our moments. We lose the connection of our life's path with the eternal part of us, so that the end of our life becomes a cul-de-sac rather than a corner. This is the power of death. Instead of walking through a wide land, our life becomes a corridor. That corridor may wind but it always ends. Our vista is in a single direction. The end of the corridor is the focus of our life, and even if we ignore it, it is still there as an anti-focus. The more we try to ignore the end, the more it pulls. We are like boats being drawn downstream to the waterfall, facing upstream, engines on full blast, trying to convince ourselves that the banks are not moving past us the wrong way. Every new ill, each ache and pain, each limitation on the body of our youth reminds us of the inexorable force pulling us to our end.

Thus, death becomes the key of our lifesong. Even if it is not mentioned, it is there, just a remove or two from our thoughts. Even if we absorb ourselves in beauty – great art, wonderful nature, or the marvel of having children with a lovely partner, death is there as a constant companion. In some ways, without death, beauty is only skin-deep. If we take death out of the story, the story becomes trivial, cartoon-like and loses its traction. The higher the theme, the more it has to include death, or it is no longer our theme.

Until we accept and try to encompass death in our thoughts and philosophy, we remain children, sitting on the deck playing games but unaware of where the boat is going. The boat starts to rock and the children are jolted out of their game. Initially they hope for a simple explanation for the disturbance. They may tell each other comforting stories; they may try to ignore the buffets. But the storm is upon them and they need – they really do need – to understand what is happening. They are shocked to discover that, far from this being a temporary squall, it is actually a storm which the boat is not going to survive. They will have to jump off or go down with it. At this point, the point when they start to try to deal honestly with that reality, those children become human people.

This is the consequence of the Fall. One great piece of evidence for the reality of the Fall as the cause of death is our shock and reluctance to accept the inevitability of death. We have a perception that "this is all wrong" and "it shouldn't happen to me". We can throw ourselves into states of mind which refuse to accept death – because we know that this is not what was meant. These states of mind range from that of the numbed victim of a disaster, through post-traumatic stress, to every neurosis and expression of angst that we display. We desire truly that death should not be the end. We cling to the hope of more moments in our lives. We see in sleep the possibility of waking after a little absence. All this is the result of losing the coherence of our life of moments.

If the Fall had not occurred, death might very well still occur, but it would simply be a turn in the road and around the corner would be the rest of our existence, waiting for us to inhabit it. Death would lose its momentum or leverage, and our lives would regain their correct centre of mass – the right pivot-point – the eternal relationship we have with him who created us.

In the next chapter, I will take a slightly different tack to try to find an answer to the biblical story of the Fall. I will do it by looking at one of the story themes found throughout scripture.

CHAPTER THREE

Two or Three Journeys to Jerusalem

Throughout the Bible we find a theme of gifts being brought to a king in Jerusalem.

In the last book of the Old Testament we read:

Then the LORD will have men who will bring offerings in righteousness and the offerings of Judah and Jerusalem will be acceptable to the Lord, as in days gone by, as in former years.

Malachi 3:3,4

These gifts are in the form of offerings – thank offerings from the people of Israel, tributes from conquered peoples and help offerings for the poor. There is a record from the earliest time in the Bible that Abram gave a tithe to Melchizedek, the king of Jerusalem. Then and onward, Jerusalem was a focus of offerings given to God, sacrifices and aid for the poor.

To reach Jerusalem there was always a climb up to the mountain of the Lord – the citadel where David built his castle. This came to be the place where the Songs of Ascents were sung as a celebratory climax to what was often a long journey. These journeys were the pilgrimages of their day. From the days of the exile, we have reliable records of Psalms of longing for the journey to Jerusalem; these songs resonate strongly with us as we travel to the heart of our beliefs. The writers of the Bible think of Jerusalem as the centre; journeys to Jerusalem represent journeys of discovery about God. The journey to the promised land, the return from exile, the recovery of the Ark of the Covenant by David, the journey of Abraham from Ur, even the journey of the Queen of Sheba – all these are used in the Old Testament to represent our own journeys of discovery and faith.

When we reach the New Testament, the theme continues, and is brought to its highest meaning. The journey of Joseph and Mary to Bethlehem is the first tale, but it is swiftly followed by the journey of the Magi bringing gifts, and the journey to and from Egypt to escape Herod. Perhaps the journey of the Magi is the start of our chain; royal visitors who bring tribute to the infant Christ to show his mastery over the kingdoms of the world. Their journey is long, and not without difficulty. It is costly, and requires faith in the signs of the nativity. Although the infant Christ is the goal of the trek, he himself has not come of age, or indeed fulfilled his purpose. There needs to be a further unfolding of the theme.

We find this in the journey of Jesus to Jerusalem with his disciples. There is a reluctance on the part of the disciples to accept the need for this: surely it places him in unnecessary danger? Yet Jesus, who in some ways does not completely know the consequences of this journey, takes the step of faith in his Father's will, and goes to confront the Jews with his infant kingdom of twelve men. He does understand the risks of confrontation with the remnant of Judah, and prophesies his resurrection in the picture of the Temple being rebuilt in three days.

The next link is made by Luke in an eyewitness account in the book of Acts. Paul, acting on an impulse from the Spirit, starts from Greece, and collects gifts for the saints in Jerusalem from the young churches along his route. There is particular emphasis on this in some of Paul's letters – especially to the Corinthians. Paul takes the gifts, and as he nears the end of the journey, receives warnings from godly Christians along the way, telling him of the consequences of his plan. Like Jesus, Paul is not sure what the end will be, but feels that this journey is essential.

In some ways, this is the culminating story of scripture, because the end of the tale is Paul being sent to Rome, and thus ends the historical line of the story of the New Testament. This story seems to have a significance all of its own, and shows the most sharply-defined images of what the kingdom that Jesus started was doing, and the issues that were of importance in the last days of the biblical record. This final recollection must contain a most important message about what a Christian is. The message moves with Paul across the sea to Rome.

What then is the crux of the message that Paul brings to the Jews?

It is there in Acts 23:6: "I stand on trial because of my hope in the resurrection of the dead."

There is almost no other argument put forward by Paul to justify his allegiance to Jesus.

A week later, Paul tells King Agrippa that he is "saying nothing more than the prophets and Moses said would happen – that Christ would suffer and as the first to rise from the dead would proclaim the light to his own people and the Gentiles".

This is the first message.

It is not to do with morality, behaviour or ritual. It is not to do with discipleship or charity for the poor. It is not even primarily to do with substitutionary sacrifice.

It is a simple proposition that there is a hope, based on reliable witness, that there is now a resurrection from the dead for all people. It is a repetition of the narrative of the empty tomb and the appearance of Christ afterwards. It is the specific call for every individual who hears the message to consider what resurrection would mean for them, and, having decided to believe that it is going to happen, to so arrange every part of their lives in congruence with that belief.

In one sense, this is the final word in scripture. There is almost no need for anything else!

- We are all born, and we find out that we are going to die. We all act throughout our lives with that in the back of our minds.
- We hear the gospel which states that one man rose after death, and that we can rise again as well.
- We make a decision to take this as our hope, and act in accordance with that belief.
- Every act that we perform after that point, which takes as its premise the belief in the resurrection, is an act of faith.
- Every act that we perform which derives from a belief that death is actually the end is a failure of faith.

29

There were many words written in scripture and out of it after Paul's declaration to the Jews. We continue to churn out advice to both Christians and non-Christians about how to live, and what it is all about. We concentrate on many topics which help us understand our faith. There is a lot of theology around!

Nevertheless, a Christian is one who believes Christ got up and lived after being killed. That belief, if it is real, will change everything we think and do, and there is (almost) nothing more that is ultimately needed.

CHAPTER FOUR

The Fabric of Our Lives

I want to look more closely at the structure of our eternal being! In the first chapter I wrote that our life is a single entity with no division. I stated that this life includes our origin, trajectory and termination. I used the word 'termination' rather than 'death' because I did not want to confuse two things which are commonly confused. I wanted to retain the term death to describe spiritual death – that is, separation of our being from its true source. Conventionally, of course, death is simply seen as the last point in time at which we are considered to be alive. I have instead called this 'termination', to emphasise that this point is not a limitation of existence; it is more like an edge of our being. To explain this further, I might say that we all have a height. We are limited by an upper boundary – the top of our head. This boundary defines us in one sense, but it does not affect our actual existence. Our height is our termination in the vertical direction. Our death is similar to our height; it simply is our termination in the direction of time.

Having looked at our life as origin, trajectory and termination, I find it helpful to fill out these rather dull words with a picture of our life as a cloth being woven on a loom. The analogy helps me to describe a view of our eternal life.

The loom supports threads running along (warp) and across (weft) the fabric. In carpet weaving, additional threads are woven into the warp and weft to make a design.

Figure 9. A loom with warp and weft.

Let us suppose that the warp represents our nature, that is, the things about us that we bring into this world. These threads run all the way through our lives, and give our personality shape, and determine our reactions and actions, and also our history.

Let us further suppose that the weft describes our nurture, and the effects of the passage of time, our upbringing and all that the world can throw at us.

Let us lastly suppose that, as in carpet weaving, the coloured threads are things that we make decisions about – acts of our own will. These are supported by the other two threads of nurture and nature.

In our mind's eye, we can follow the course of the shuttle taking one thread of nurture (all the threads together are called the weft, but a single thread is known as a 'pick') across the fabric of our lives. The thread weaves up and down, interacting with all the strands of our nature (warps). As the thread progresses, coloured threads of our own decisions are woven into the network of warp and weft thus formed. The process coalesces separate strands into one entity, forming a pattern, possibly a beautiful design. The joining of two dimensions of threads in an interlocking pattern with the interwoven coloured threads is an act of creation, just as the unfolding of our lives is an act of creation. Some parts of the pattern are predetermined, but there is also a mystery of transition from individual crossings of threads and interwoven coloured threads to a new and complete picture revealed when we stand back from the loom and look at the whole thread crossing the cloth in its formation. If this is a true picture, we can rightly say that we make a genuinely original contribution to God's world – ourselves!

I wish to now apply this picture to give a perspective on resurrection.

Let us suppose that this life we are living represents just one thread of the weft (a pick). The pick begins at our birth, and ends at our physical death. In between are represented all our nature (every warp thread), all our nurture (the passage of the weft thread), and all our decisions made at every stage of our life (the interwoven coloured threads). In one sense this picture contains the whole of our earthly life as we see it now.

Is this complete? Of course not: it is only one pick!

Without all the other weft threads, the picture is incomplete. Our whole life appears complete between birth and death, and yet, as this picture shows, our existence is much more than one thread. This 'pick' has become disconnected from the completed cloth. Because of the Fall, the one thread we are living through in this life is our complete earthly experience – termination of the pick may be all that we ever have. My conviction is that our reconciliation with Christ in his death and resurrection allows us to reconnect with the whole pattern of our existence, and become a complete cloth.

My belief is that our present life is just the first pick of many, and that as we enter the resurrection life, we start a process that will continue for eternity – the weaving of a 'cloth' to give glory to God.

The Bayeux tapestry is two hundred and thirty-one feet long and must contain more than ten thousand wefts, and yet our eternal life's tapestry will overwhelm this completely!

Interlude

We have now viewed our relationship with eternity in a way that allows us to start to see how our present lives might link into an eternal economy. There are formidable difficulties in comprehending eternity as the container to our lives: as we live inside the container, it is hard to get a good look at it! Over the years, these difficulties have prompted controversial ideas about how to practically deal with a God who is "yesterday, today, forever". The biblical record shows evidence of a development of human understanding (not always chronological) as different people grappled with mysteries of death and time. It seems clear that Jesus' teachings were recorded from a resurrectionist (pharisaic) viewpoint. The early church fathers were forced to engage with concepts of predestination and fate and free will as they came into missionary contact with the Greek, Roman, African and Asian worlds. Some of the ideas that they were forced to decide upon are so powerful that the church divided denominationally across different ways of seeing God's nature and activity. It is quite true that mystery is an overwhelming characteristic of God's presence. I have therefore taken the bold step of continuing to develop the picture of our lives as fabric in an attempt to relate to some of these knotty doctrines. Although they divide opinion and even denominations, the issues they relate to remain relevant to the modern world. People want to know where they fit into the universe; they also want to know if their decisions and actions make a difference to their fate. I have concentrated on the concept of destiny as a way of grasping the impact of eternity on our lives now, as well as it being our ultimate destination. I found that this needed four chapters to itself.

Best of luck!

CHAPTER FIVE

Total Depravity

What then is time? If no one asks me, I know what it is. If I wish to explain it to him who asks, I do not know.

Saint Augustine

The Reformed or Calvinistic doctrine of Predestination includes the doctrines of Total Depravity, Unconditional Election, Limited Atonement, Irresistible Grace and Perseverance of the Saints. They are commonly referred to using their initials (TULIP). They continue to be a stumbling block for many in their understanding of Christian Reformed doctrine.

Typically, the two sides of the argument fall out over whether our God is perfectly fair as well as perfectly just. This is linked to whether man has truly been given free will to choose to be redeemed, or actually man has little part to play in the matter, God having decided the outcome of a life 'before' it ever occurred.

It is common to find Calvinists holding to uncomfortably strict views on this issue for fear that we might water down scripture into a group of social platitudes, and Liberals outraged at the possibility that God is some sort of sick scientist who creates Frankenstein creatures only to throw them onto the rubbish tip when they turn out wrong. Traditional evangelical teaching is seen as different from post-evangelical belief, and often causes division in churches.

I hope that a more mature view of eternal life may re-shade these old battle lines into the structural elements of a redemptive process both loving and just!

If we approach these doctrines using the fabric structure as a picture of an eternal life in the making, we may assess them as descriptors of the human condition.

In these four chapters I will look at each part of the TULIP doctrines in relation to this thesis of eternal life.

1) Total Depravity

John Calvin used the term 'Total Depravity' to mean that, despite the ability of people to outwardly uphold the law, "there [remains] an inward distortion which makes all human actions displeasing to God, whether or not they are outwardly good or bad".[8]

If we examine the woven structure I suggested in the last chapter, we can see that the warp threads of our existence (our nature) are likely to contain the inward distortion that this doctrine talks about. Our nature contains the elements of our structure which being human bestows upon us. We cannot choose our parentage, race or species. In one sense these elements are not 'our fault'. Total Depravity implies that these threads of our being are part of our 'cloth', and, left to us, the depravity will come out in the wash, whatever we do.

Total Depravity means that the weft threads of nurture are also distorted, by the warp threads of our nature. Thus, without outside help, even the very best things that happen to us throughout our lives will still result in a distorted fabric in our resultant personality.

In my illustration, the third sort of thread – the interspersed coloured elements representing our own freely-willed input and intentions – is also bent out of shape by the distorted warp and weft. These freely-willed threads are indeed 'our fault' (unlike the 'nature' threads). When we weave our free will into our cloth, we may intend the best, but the distorted framework of nurture and nature distort our best into the same old patterns that our nature dictates. Paul makes a

---

[8] Quote from Muller, Richard A.; *Calvin and the Reformed Tradition (ed.)*; Grand Rapids, MI: Baker Academic (2012), p.51.

famously frustrated groan in Romans: "Wretched man that I am! Who will deliver me from this body of death?"[9] Some have wrongly concluded that this cry leads us to a classical Greek idea of impure body versus pure soul. As we will see, this is not true; a further separation of body from soul is not the remedy for this condition! Redemption is of body and soul together; resurrection is resurrection of the complete human, not simply a paltry part.

The Calvinist doctrine of Total Depravity correctly assumes that we have the privilege of free choice so as to take the credit and the blame for our own actions. This is important, because we are not automata who sin or cannot sin by design. If we were automata, there would be no particular goodness or badness in the decisions we took, because 'deciding' would be an illusion. The reason that it is fair and just to judge humans as sinful despite the fact that their badness is 'natural badness' is that it is not just one misplaced thread in a garment that is the problem; it is the whole warp and weft that is distorted. God is not unfair to condemn the fabric for being distorted – he is actually simply stating the truth: the fabric will never be fit to wear unless the distortion is removed. Even the nice coloured threads of our good-willed intentions are not nice to look at as a whole life's worth – they are woven into a crooked mess by the underlying fabric. The remedy is to rehang the warp threads onto a different loom, thus changing the nature of the human. It is my judgement that this change, although major, does not change the human into something completely different. A different nature (gained, obviously, from Christ) does not change our 'nurtural' history – that remains, but it falls into a better position. In the same way, the rehanging of the cloth will reset our freely-willed pattern of coloured threads into the intrinsically good pattern that it should be. This rehanging does not discard any part of the cloth. Redemption, as stated above, is Redemption of the whole man.

Why is the decision to believe in the resurrection so central?

It is important to note that there is a freely-willed decision to allow the 'rehanging of the cloth' onto Christ's loom. In effect, one of the threads that we specifically control, being neither nurture nor nature, determines whether we allow our cloth to be rehung. As I stated above,

---

[9] Romans 7:23-25 (ESV).

the change is major. It might seem that when the whole nature of a man is rejigged, that man ceases to exist. It might seem that this particular decision is so major as to amount to suicide. However, I would reiterate my conviction that this change does not destroy the human; on the contrary, it reforms our self into the proper person we should be.

The particular thread of free will which allows the change of loom is the decision to believe or not to believe. It is fascinating to ponder the effect of 'believe it or not'. Specifically, that belief is the belief that although Jesus physically died, he became alive again some seventy-two hours later. To think that believing this specific statement could be the trigger to the rehanging of our human nature requires some explanation. Why this particular shibboleth? Is it some sort of password or ritual mental exercise with a random code for the initiate?

Firstly, it is evident that the mechanism of this Redemption is a mystery. I hope that the chapters I have written so far will allow the reader to agree with me that unless we were sitting in eternity, with a perspective of the whole of time, we would not be able to understand what happens here. We live in the auditorium of a shadow-theatre, and what we see at present is merely the projection of eternal processes onto the screen of our perception. To peep behind the screen is not possible for us – it would destroy the perception!

Secondly, the will to believe in one thing (the resurrection of Christ) is a trigger. Without this trigger, it seems that God has self-limited to respect the boundary that our humanity sets. With the trigger released, the door unlocks, and it allows an entire reinvention of our life's structure. The specific belief is related to the reinvention in two ways. First, the object of the belief, the person of Jesus Christ, is the template for our reinvention, and in some way our new nature is moulded over Christ's nature into its new form. Second, the belief relates to resurrection. This specific element seems to be necessary for the self-limiting Deity to link our own old life, which loses coherence at death, into the new life that does not.

I am afraid these are the only two clues I can proffer to explain why believing in Christ's resurrection is essential to the process of Redemption.

I conclude this look into the first TULIP doctrine, that of Total Depravity, by a short note. It seems useful to point out that the warp threads that my illustration paints our nature to be are threads that run throughout our whole lives. They span us from birth to death. In changing them, things are changed not only in the present (easy to comprehend), but also in the future (which requires some faith) and, challengingly, in the past (which requires some thought to come to terms with).

This difficulty of seeing our Redemption as acting on our whole lives – past, present and future – is matched by the difficulty of comprehending that our original sin also affects our whole life from a time even before we were born – "I was born a sinner."[10] This balance of understanding may help in the process of acceptance of things that we cannot really grasp! I wish you the best of grace as we continue this journey through the rest of the tulip beds.

---

[10] Psalm 51:5 (NLT)

CHAPTER SIX

Unconditional Election

2) Unconditional Election

Unconditional Election describes the view that – put simply – God decides who goes to heaven. The teeth of the doctrine lie in the helplessness of man to influence God's decision to save us. In effect, the doctrine says that nothing in our nature and no act we do, including our efforts to believe, can convince God to change his ultimate plan for each of us. This strikes people as very unfair, as we have a strong motivation and instinct to try to protect ourselves and guarantee our safe futures (self-preservation). We naturally feel that an action on our part should make some difference to our future. This is intensified by the apparent heartlessness of a Deity who troubles to create us individually and then apparently discards us regardless of our being, identity, uniqueness and selfhood.

It is clear how time-dependent this doctrine is, as it attempts to look at the actions and decisions of the eternal God from the perspective of a human within his or her lifetime. The structure of nurture, nature and free will which I have described can, I think, square this circle, and bridge the gap between God's sovereignty and our sense of justice. The way I would approach it is by considering three questions:

> a) What is God 'looking' at when he makes his unconditional elective choice?

My contention is that in the context of this doctrine, God is looking at the completed human being (warp, weft and freely-willed pattern) that I have described. We see a small cross-section of our being during any day, or indeed year, of our lives. Our knowledge of our past life is mediated by physical memory, contained in our brains. There is a wealth of detail about 'us' that is not apparent when we consider our deservedness to receive salvation from the eternal God. This God definitely created each one of us, but the result of that creation is developed over our lifetime. In the sense that God placed free will in each of us, the creation that is 'us' is outside God's control. In another sense – that of God's sovereign authorship of the arena in which we exist – that creation *is* within his control. This doctrine looks at God's complete sovereign authorship, not at the free will contained in our being. The coexistence of elements within and without God's control is paradoxical, but no more so than quantum physical effects such as the wave-particle duality of the electron.

Effectively, this doctrine considers God the Creator looking at a completed human, including all the events of that human's life, all the decisions which that human made, and indeed the nature of that human – inherited and imposed. This is God looking at the first completed weft (a pick) running across all the warp threads of a life. This also includes all the freely-willed decisions which that human ever made, including the decision to believe in him! The decision that God is making is not within a life, it is outside that life. God is pictured as 'reacting to' that human, as we might react to a smell or taste – we know immediately whether we like it or not. In Unconditional Election, God decides about the 'whole person', not primarily considering each individual part of the human, or limiting his knowledge to any one time in their life.

b) What are we doing when we try to earn salvation?

The injustice of this doctrine also appears if we consider it only from a day-to-day perspective. We do something good for a neighbour, and naturally we want that to make a difference to our destiny. We feel guilty about an act we did last week, and we try to make amends. To have a God who gives us a fail mark when our life has ended, regardless of those specific things, seems to be wrong. This is not, however, the appropriate perspective from which to consider this part of God.

However hard it is, this level of thinking will not answer problems related to free will and eternal destiny. This is because the individual time-based acts and events are not 'disentangleable' when looking at an eternal decision by Deity about salvation. In one sense, the decision of Unconditional Election cannot unpick a human; it is a decision about a composite whole. It is 'not allowed' to consider individual threads of the weave. This is certainly not to say that the weave is not important; it is the only thing we have to work on during our lives. It is just to say that this one particular aspect of God's nature is irrelevant to 'doing good works', or 'coming from the right stock' or even 'making the best of the day'.

  c) Does God have free will, and do we?

It is right to now consider whether God can 'freely will'. Is he able to choose wrongly, or does his nature forbid it?

Of course, you can see now the trap we have fallen into; it is the problem that God is outside and beyond our capacity to grasp. We can only see his justice in our human terms. We find ourselves judging God by our lights, treating him as some sort of superhuman like a Norse god. When we think of God 'choosing', we inevitably suppose that he approaches a choice with our combination of ignorance as to the result, in the hope of a good one and fear of a bad one! A moment of thought shows that a God outside time does not have these thoughts and feelings. To him, things 'are or are not'. He sees the results and the composites from behind and before, and before and after. A decision is 'anticipated', 'made' and 'remembered' as one whole.

When seen from God's perspective, what are our freely-willed choices? I think that the coloured threads interspersed through a carpet give as good a picture as any! We weave them one by one, latching on to our fortunes and our selfhood, and God sees all of them as they relate to each other and to our nurture and our nature. We come back to the second key mentioned in the chapter on 'resurrection', where there is automaticity about decisions seen from a perspective of hindsight ("I can see now that I was always going to be...")

So, to summarise, I find that the uncomfortable doctrine of Unconditional Election springs from the nature of God, looked at from the perspective of our eternal destiny. From that perspective, God's 'foreknowing in full possession of the facts' can be mistaken for him 'deciding while not knowing the future' – in this case, about our eternal destiny. Far from taking the responsibility for our choices away from us, Deity looks at the completed human life as a whole, inclusive of all freely-willed decisions, our fortunes and our natural tendencies, and offers the grace of Christ to those whom he knows have truly wished for it. In some ways, I feel that this doctrine is unhelpful because it can imply things that are not so, if taken in the wrong context. Having said that, the correct response to God's loving election of a believer is, will be and always has been eternal thanks.

CHAPTER SEVEN

Limited Atonement and Irresistible Grace

We will now look at the third and fourth of the doctrines which Calvinists are said to hold dear.

3) Limited Atonement

It seems that Calvin himself may not have expressed Limited Atonement in the way that many Reformed scholars would. In effect, Limited Atonement states that Christ's sacrifice is sufficient to save everybody, but is only given to a limited number of people – those whom God chooses, based very much on the sovereign choice of Deity described in the previous chapter. This limitation is the point of controversy between Arminian and Reformed theologians. How can God limit his salvation to those he chooses without apparently taking account of their freely-willed choices? In fact, this objection is very similar, if not identical semantically, to the objection to Unconditional Election.

If we look at God as a limited being making a choice, as a judge might in court, this doctrine is fraught with unfairness. If we see God's choice as taking place 'behind and before, above and below, before, during and after' the human life, we will see that there is a necessary sovereignty about God's decision to save some and not others, which stems from his nature (all-knowing and all-powerful), but does not in any way reduce the power of our free choice. To extend the comments in the previous chapter, God sees a human as an artist does a canvas, but a canvas which is painted over the course of a lifetime. In some ways, the canvas is simply a preliminary draft of the eternal creature, but that is not the point here. As in the loom analogy, 'the canvas itself' adds some strokes of colour to the painting, these strokes representing our free choices. These are outside God's power but within the framework of time over which we are stretched. God's choice to limit atonement to the elect is made both with the whole canvas 'in hand', and also throughout the formation of the canvas, with all our unique choices clearly showing within the whole. This 'choice' is an evolving, reactive and responsive act of God's Spirit – dividing joint and sinew (!) and is completely fair, just and expressive of love. Jesus' sacrificial atonement is applied as a direct expression of that choice.

It seems to me that whatever our sinful nature is, the atonement is sufficient; whatever our faulty nurture has been, Jesus' love is still directed at us; and whatever our millions of freely-willed choices are or will be, every one of them is reflected in the one summatory choice we are offered: "Do you or do you not believe in Christ who rose from the dead?"

4) Irresistible Grace

Irresistible Grace, the fourth Reformed doctrine, is often contrasted to Prevenient Grace, which is the Arminian (and Wesleyan) alternative view. In effect, these deal with when and how God's grace is given to humans. The first version, following on from the previous three doctrines, emphasises divine choice as to who will or will not accept that grace. God is said to choose the human and, thereafter, that human has very little say in the matter. The second version merely states that God loves everybody and offers his grace to all who freely choose to accept it. This obviously puts the onus on the human to choose to accept God.

As with the other doctrines, we can see that the disagreement between these two depends largely on the tense of the verbs used! If grace was given *in the past* (before humans existed), then that implies either that God decides who will accept that grace in advance and creates us with that in mind, or that God doesn't really know and throws it out there for the human to respond to. Either way, it implies that God is limited (in knowledge or in the ability to give us a truly free choice).

If God gives the grace in the future, the 'decision' is made after the human is created. This implies that God is either unfair or limited in power.

You will see that if we look at a human as a composite of nature, nurture and freely-willed choices spun out over a lifetime, this will to a large extent blur the tenses. If we look at God as an eternally present being holding our loom in his view, we can catch a glimpse of his perspective, which offers grace freely to those souls he chooses, with no coercion upon that soul to accept it, while also knowing the response of the soul to the gracious offer. In this way, I believe, most reasonable people (with a little jump of faith to imagine the unimaginable!) can see that fairness can coexist with ultimate sovereignty in the eternal court of God! Sometimes we sympathise with Alice in discussion with the Red Queen:

> *"There's no use trying," she said: "one can't believe impossible things." "I daresay you haven't had much practice," said the Queen. "When I was your age, I always did it for half-an-hour a day. Why, sometimes I've believed as many as six impossible things before breakfast."*[11]

---

[11] Lewis Carroll; *Through the Looking-Glass and What Alice Found There;* (1871).

CHAPTER EIGHT

Gilding the Tulip

Moving on from the Calvinist view.

5) Perseverance of the Saints

The last of the reformed doctrines noted here is Perseverance of the Saints. This, like the other four we have considered, emphasises the monergistic side to salvation (the God-determined side). By this teaching, when a saint has been chosen and has been given grace, there is no way in which God's will can be undone. Of course not; God is all-powerful! Arminians will prefer to emphasise the human role in freely choosing to believe, thus 'allowing' God to give us his grace – and of course, possibly backsliding at a later date, and even, conceivably, rejecting that grace entirely.

I hope that, rather than arguing as an Arminian, a Lutheran or a Calvinist (or as a Roman Catholic), the structure that I have pictured may allow us to imagine that God's sovereignty and man's free will are interfaced perfectly across our 'cloth' by threads of our nurture and nature interwoven with the colours inserted by our freely-willed choices. As the grace of God brings Christ's perfect nature into us, the threads of our nature warp back into the perfection that God has promised us. These threads are part of our structure, and persist all the way through, or across, our lives. The work of grace cannot be considered finished until all the warps are 'warped', until we die! Thus, while we live, the uncertainty of our present existence remains.

It may be objected that to accept both the sovereignty of God and the free will of man in the same life makes it hard to know where one stands. Are we certain of our fate, or do we have to maintain an agnostic safety net when asked about the future?

The answer to this question is contained in the structure I have described, and allows us to behave correctly in our time-based decisions. If we are asking for an insurance policy to protect us from the effects of deliberately and persistently living in a way that contradicts the command to love, we cannot expect it! If we do this, then we weave threads into our cloth that no Redemption of our nature (re-warping of the loom) can improve. What we do has a real influence on our completed self, and there is a real pain which we all experience when we deliberately go against the new nature that we have embraced. This is the true expression of conscience, and is real evidence of the continuing work of the Spirit in our lives.

Someone may then ask, "What is the consequence of sinning after we have made a decision to believe?" Throughout the ages there have been countless attempts by different churches to handle the failure of convinced Christians to live in love. They range from penances to regular confession, weekly reciting of the liturgy, giving sacrificial gifts and include psychological interventions such as counselling and contemplation. In past ages, people purchased 'pardons', or used relics and pilgrimages which they mistakenly believed would earn their forgiveness (or, perhaps more reasonably, to demonstrate their repentance). The existence of an industry based on guilt is indeed a major criticism of the church by humanists of all sorts. I hope that this chapter can persuade you that there is no need for any such time-limited remedies, neither does scripture require them.

If you are a Christian (or indeed any person with a morality or sense of justice that bases itself on love) with any insight and honesty, you will have struggled with your own failure many times in the past, and hopefully will continue that struggle in the future! Examples of questions that are often thought of by serious Christians include: What is the effect of sin 'after Redemption'? How many times can we sin and repent before it is too late? What is an 'unforgivable sin'? I am not going to comprehensively quote the wealth of advice, counsel, doctrine and teaching on this issue! I will instead make three points.

a) The issue of sin for believers is largely the same issue as Perseverance of the Saints.

It is a relevant and current topic of daily interest for everyone who wishes to actually live as a 'lover'. The differences between Calvinist and Arminian doctrines are reflected in our own hearts every time we look at the aftermath of a sin in our lives. Am I 'still saved'? Can I assume Irresistibility of Grace? Am I actually a Perseverant Saint? The debate goes on (or should!) every time our errant will cuts across the lines of loving behaviour we could have followed. The remedy for this internal debate is to be found in the same place as the debate between theologians about Calvin's doctrine – outside time, and with the first eternal man, Jesus Christ. Note that the doctrine of Perseverance of the Saints is only to be used by the believer as an internal and personal reflection on God's perspective on their sin. It is never to be used as some sort of quality marker of a particular denomination or sect which has taken the pharisaic line that only they can judge whether someone is accepted by God!

b) Scripture provides relevant advice for us, making clear that the problem is significant and has been central since the first days of the church.

Some passages are clear about the significance of our actions, e.g. Galatians 6:7: "Do not be deceived: God cannot be mocked. Whatever a man sows, he will reap in return."

Some give encouragement that these decisions are important to God, and there is help, e.g. 1 Corinthians 10:13: "No temptation has seized you except what is common to man. And God is faithful; He will not let you be tempted beyond what you can bear. But when you are tempted, He will also provide an escape, so that you can stand up under it."

Others imply that there is perennial forgiveness, e.g. Matthew 18:21-22: "Then Peter came to Jesus and asked, 'Lord, how many times shall I forgive my brother who sins against me? Up to seven times?' Jesus answered, 'I tell you, not just seven times, but seventy-seven times!'"

These quotes show that there is an issue here that does not allow certainty or thoughtless dogmatism! This should not concern us.

Uncertainty is absolutely par for the course, but it is a limited uncertainty. This uncertainty is in the nature of things, and will be considered in the next chapter.

The final and most pertinent quote shows the balance between uncertainty and certainty that is a living dramatization of the word 'faith'. It shows that the process of faith includes the consideration of all the facts available, the admission of inability to get through the blockage, and is the final resort to a determination to act positively despite the incompleteness (not absence!) of knowledge. It is found in Romans 7:21-27: "So this is the principle I have discovered: When I want to do good, evil is right there with me. For in my inner being I delight in God's Law. But I see another law at work in my body, warring against the law of my mind and holding me captive to the law of sin that dwells within me. What a wretched man I am! Who will rescue me from this body of death? Thanks be to God, through Jesus Christ our Lord! So then, with my mind I serve the law of God, but with my flesh I serve the law of sin."

> c) Scripture and Christian teaching do not allow a quantitative 'counting up' of sins, with an overall assessment on a human level (statistical or legal!)

It is here that the Calvinist doctrine is clearest and most helpful. Judgement belongs to God and him alone. The picture of our life as a completed entity, not seen in time, not seen in part but judged as a whole in the fair light of eternity, is the one I wish to paint for you. While we remain within time and space, our faith in God's ability to save should result in us acting in a manner that can only be justified by certainty. We can confidently live and act through faith as if the salvation we expect in eternity is, in fact, available right here and now.

We can both see on a practical level that the Arminian view does describe the apparent loss of faith in those we thought were 'saved', but also that it does not erase the doctrine of Perseverance which allows us to exercise our right to trust that the Almighty God, once he has chosen, never lets us go. We live both in the flashlight of the present moment and also in the noonday sunshine of our eternal life.

This concludes my treatment of the Reformed (Calvinist) view, and as we leave it, I suggest that the Calvinist perspective on God's sovereignty should be more widely considered. There is a sheer wonder that is expressed in these thoughts, at a God who decides with no one to gainsay. That this should appear to diminish human influence on God's purpose is, as we can understand, natural. When we look at God from this perspective, we see 'The Almighty' – unchangeable and massive, powerfully creating the new heavens and earth, reclaiming what he wishes from the wreckage of failed attempts to live outside the law of love. That he 'decides' not to save some things is logical necessity – and God is the author of loving logic. We must respond to a perception of a God who acts outside our idea of love, but we must also be ready to discover the reality of love – what love really is – despite our time-based worries to the contrary.

"All shall be well, and all manner of thing shall be well."[12] But we only see and feel a faint shadow now of what really is. To say that we cannot know at present must not dissuade us from trying to know, and there is wisdom to be found even in the foolishness of God.

---

[12] Julian of Norwich (1342-1416).

Interlude

We have looked at the human life from the perspective of the eternal, which has drawn us into the Reformed doctrines which naturally take that viewpoint. I now wish to bring us back to the human side of the eternal universe.

We live within the confines of time and space, and they frame our lives and our thoughts. Inevitably we are limited by this frame, not seeing outside it. This brings uncertainty where God has certainty, and doubt where God sees the reality.

The final chapters are written to describe the situation where we possess a box, locked and containing a truth. At present we have no key, but we are tempted to break open the box and discover what is within. Should we do it? Schrodinger's famous cat which is both alive and dead at the same time is surprisingly relevant to our state of doubt!

Before dealing with these issues, I would note that uncertainty and doubt are features of a time-based existence which will only persist in that context. By their nature, they are temporary, as well as temporal. It is common to wrongly assume that doubt is the opposite of faith. This confusion may have some roots in nomenclature and nuance of meaning. I would like to be quite clear that doubt is *not* the opposite of faith. This position is correct because it is clear that faith cannot not be defined as the absence of doubt. If that were the case, then faith would be the synonym of certainty. We know that it is not!

Instead, it is useful to see faith as more than a state of mind, either in terms of knowledge or in terms of emotional reaction. Faith is the first action in which we interface with the eternal. It is helpful to see it as a bridge between the temporal and the eternal. To put it simply, here we have uncertainty, which means that doubt is normal. In eternity there will be certainty, and doubt will cease to exist. We make decisions here and now as if we lived in eternity, despite our clear position of temporality. As the Bible puts it in 1 Corinthians 13:12, "For now we see in a mirror, dimly, but then we will see face to face. Now I know only in part; then I will know fully, even as I have been fully known."

CHAPTER NINE

Uncertainty – A Note

After looking at some doctrines relating to destiny we see that Christians still find difficulty with the unknown. A major example of this is seen resulting from 'free will'. Free will implies by its very name that a choice is made freely. The freedom of this choice precludes prior knowledge of its outcome. The outcome is therefore unknown until the choice is made. Reformed theology gets around man's free will by saying that although its results are unknown to man, they are already known to God; actually, through this knowledge, God has 'already' made up his mind about which of us he has saved, and which he has not. In contrast to this, Arminians look at the other side of the coin and put more emphasis on the temporal choices made by man, with God voluntarily (gracefully) submitting to the choice of a mortal to accept or reject grace. This does not necessarily help completely, for we are still left with the mystery of why people make choices in the way they do. It is possible to rationally hold the view that there are no free choices at all because we are creatures of instinct and are psychologically programmed from birth. In this view, the fabric illustration I have used does not have any 'free-will threads' – we may be a simple warp and weft of nature interleaved with nurture. We become much more like complicated, but basically predictable, robots. Even if this is the case, we remain complex enough to prevent the determinist from explaining everything about us; we rarely willingly behave as though our actions were pre-determined – even if we hold a determinist philosophy ourselves.

There is a mystery of complexity here which may be portrayed using a visual illustration. It is quite possible to look at a computer screen very closely and see individual dots composing the picture. Each dot can be explained as a piece of electrical information, separate from the rest of the dots on the screen. If you draw back to look at a million tiny dots at once, however, a picture emerges which has no relation at all to the close analysis of the reasons the dots are individually produced.

Figure 10. Pixels making a picture.

We can digitise all visual information that our eyes can see (that is, reduce its complexity to make it possible to show on a screen), but the opposite process (that of explaining the picture that we plainly perceive) is harder than the digitisation. The picture requires a different level of explanation from the dots.

In the illustration I have given, I am sure that the scientific rules governing conservation of information and entropy are followed; nevertheless, the point of the illustration is to show that complexity leads to the emergence of unexpected patterns 'heterodyned' on to simple material. Because of this, I suggest that even if you are a determinist who argues that everything is strictly controlled by its prior causes, practically speaking we are still beings who have free will! The consequences of free will are explained in different ways by Reformed and Arminian scholars, as we have seen.

The problem is not whether the Reformed or Arminian scholars are right about free will (I hope that this thesis about the application of grace being outside time may help encourage the view that a satisfying answer is conceivable). No, the problem is the unknown itself. "The whole creation waits..."[13] – with bated breath. Uncertainty has remained the crux of our difficulty, whether we are theologians, mathematicians of chaos theory, quantum physicists, gay rights activists, people bereaved, gamblers, students waiting for a result, statisticians or even plain evangelicals wondering whether they can pitch camp and stand firm.

If there is one difficulty related to uncertainty in Calvinist theology, there are ten difficulties of a similar nature in our everyday lives. Uncertainty is so pervasive that it appears to be part of the very nature of the temporal universe our minds inhabit. It is also likely that to be human in this world, it is necessary for that human to 'live and breathe doubt', as I have written elsewhere. Even determinist philosophers find difficulty with uncertainty. Chaos theory and the uncertainty principle both provide fairly healthy obstacles to anyone who says that they can predict the future, or even state reliably what is happening in a different location from the observer.

Uncertainty forces us to either leave an issue alone, or to choose an outcome. Uncertainty is very often related to the passage of time ("What will happen tomorrow?"). This is not always the case, though; some doubt is present when we use any of our senses to examine a person or even an object (for example, "Is this a good hazelnut?"). We do not know what will happen tomorrow. We do not know the contents of a nut. If we follow the theory of relativity, we understand that the space-time continuum is structured in such a way that it is not conceivable to know, at any particularly moment, anything at a distance with certainty! To know, we need to interact. Interaction requires transfer of information. Information requires energy. Energy is transmitted by electromagnetic radiation. This cannot travel faster than light. We therefore cannot even know what actually is happening around the corner until it is 'old news'. Looked at in this way, distance and time are the same thing – a barrier to certainty.

It is clear that we are always living with uncertainty, and have developed practical ways to get around these barriers to knowledge.

---

[13] Romans 8:18-20 (CEB).

The first way to surmount uncertainty I have termed 'encompassing'.

To illustrate this, consider your stomach! This is located a foot from your brain (give or take), and therefore, technically, we cannot 'know' what is happening there. This technicality is obviated by the fact that our brain and stomach are linked by many nerves, so we consider the stomach to be part of 'ourselves'. When we deal with our stomach, we have to deal with time periods that are longer than the time it takes for those nerves to pass messages back and forth to the brain. We don't try to have a millisecond by millisecond stomach thought! This does not work. We think about what is happening in our stomach over a matter of seconds, and this is enough. To put it another way, we truly 'know' our stomach by its feeling, and this feeling develops. If we take an instantaneous 'reading' of our feeling, we will not get the correct answer, so we need to wait. This is what I mean by 'encompassing"; we consider that our body encompasses the stomach, and we ignore the passage of time that the nerves require to inform one part about the other. We therefore assume a unity which includes lots of time lapses. In one way, we allow the focus of our observation to blur across some time, and by doing this we get a truer picture. Mathematically, the instantaneous gradient (differential) of a graph may not give us what we need. We might get a truer picture by looking at a larger segment of the graph (taking the integral); in this example, over a period of time.

The second way to get around uncertainty is theory and recollection.

In some ways, this is an extension of 'encompassing'. We use the tools of memory, experience, ideas and theory construction to bridge the gulfs of ignorance that we are surrounded by. There is a process of blurring, and a synthesis of perceptions linked by memory. Nobody can say that these tactics give us perfect knowledge of things, and so we all practically live our lives using a series of steps of belief, or faith.

When we apply this to God, who is not immediately apparent, we are forced to use steps of faith to jump the uncertainty gaps that surround him. We look at Creation, for example, and use our experience of that to extrapolate to a Creator. This is a reasonable thing to do, as it is the way we approach all our conscious experience. In doing this, we have to accept the limitations of our theory-building, and those of our perception. We only "see through a glass darkly"[14]. This is most true when we consider God's relationship to time and space. As Creator of time and space, God must stand independently of them. This relation leads to our conception of God's power and knowledge. Both of these would seem to be unlimited by time or space, unlike our own power and knowledge. If that is so, then God's perception of uncertainty must be different from ours. Things that physics tell us are impossible in our own space-time might well be within God's power.

As an example of this, take the physical law that means we cannot know what happens at the time it happens. A star is born in the centre of the Milky Way. The speed of light means that we can only know of this birth twenty-six thousand years later. Nothing we do can reduce this time (although perhaps if we were to travel towards the light source at the speed of light, our time perception would stop, meaning that thirteen thousand years later, although no older ourselves, we would possibly see that light). We still conceive of the Milky Way as 'one unit', however. This means that we are attempting to "encompass" the galaxy. To do this, we have to blur our sense of time to ignore the twenty-six thousand years' latency. Does God do this? Does God 'contain' the galaxy, rather as we 'contain' our stomachs? I am afraid I cannot answer these questions except to say that sometimes we cannot open the box of time without misunderstanding the answer. I will repeat this in a different way: sometimes we cannot understand God because he encompasses the whole of our timespan in a single instant – to 'open the box' of that 'God instant' means that the concept becomes contaminated with other assumptions we have about time, and the results are misleading.

When it comes to God, we are in some ways trying to answer all our uncertainties in one personal being who knows the answer! The concept of this Deity as the ultimate Creator of space and time gives us a choice: it is either too difficult (and we 'make do' with a Norse god who lives a long time and is very powerful, but is ultimately limited); or it is possible, but must be understood carefully to avoid misunderstandings based on the uncertainties outlined above. It becomes important not to 'open the box' too readily unless we wish to see things that appear to

---

[14] 1 Corinthians 13:12.

contradict sense and causality, not to mention entropy. Some things only make sense in this universe if we deliberately leave the box closed. This is similar to the limitations we have on studying a dynamic system. If we dissect a frog, we find out plenty about its structure, but we cease to be able to see it interacting as a living creature.

This note on uncertainty in relation to our knowledge of God concludes by stating that sometimes it is impossible to open the box of God's mystery without changing the nature of the question we asked about that mystery, thus losing the thread of the answer. This is especially true with causality, but also includes all questions that include God's omniscience, omnipresence or ultimate power. I would sum it up by saying that if you conceive of a being that is utterly good and utterly powerful as we do when talking of God, you cannot have those two characteristics side by side within a space-time continuum. Utter goodness implies lack of freedom to be evil, while utter power requires the freedom to be either. The two cannot coexist in a conventional causal arena. They can exist outside that arena, however – where we cannot follow!

Uncertainty exists in the church in several large areas which I am going to consider in the remaining chapters, relating them as far as I can to the structures described in the book so far.

CHAPTER TEN

Uncertainty about the Word

God's commands in scripture.

When is a command not a command? When do scriptural exhortations – especially on moral issues – apply to our life in this day and age? It is often argued that culture and civilisation have moved dramatically onward since the days when scripture was written down, making large chunks of the Bible irrelevant.

It is clear that in the mainstream Christian view, the Bible was written by human agents, but as a whole should be treated as a divinely-inspired authority.

Viewed as a secular document with sixty-six books, modern critical approaches have stripped every part of scripture down into ordinary texts, edited, copied and authored for specific purposes (not necessarily for purposes that we would consider relevant to ourselves). This approach sees the words as written at a specific time, for a specific purpose. The method is analytical, and reductive; it looks at the meanings of the earliest texts and extracts sense, not just from the words, but from the political and religious context, comparable translations and the parchments themselves. Traditional comment and usage is removed from the equation as much as possible to avoid bias. The results show that when treated in this way, scripture can be criticised and defined just as any other text, and may contain inconsistencies, prejudice, errors and misleading statements.

We know that a text of any sort may serve as an inspiration, beyond any literal interpretation, original intent or meaning of the author. We see this in scripture itself, where prophetic texts reference the law and the historical texts, using them to speak into different situations and contexts. We see the New Testament integrating and building on concepts and imagery from the Old Testament. It is clear that the readers of Paul's letters had a deep understanding of the law and the prophets, which altered their understanding of the epistles themselves. Cross-referencing is almost continuous throughout the Bible, giving the text a unity which exceeds almost any other group of texts.

Beyond the perfectly normal human, temporally cogent flow of ideas (in a poetic, visionary or prophetic sense) found in scripture, it is good to try to understand the mystery of God's hand in the creation of the Bible; in other words, to try to establish the way in which divine revelation interlocks with the manuscripts.

The Bible itself has a special group of concepts surrounding 'The Word'. 'The Word' in this sense includes scripture itself; the creative power of God; the person of Christ and the divinely-inspired spoken and recorded words of men by the agency of the Holy Spirit. Vision, poetry, song and recollected history can all be 'The Word' in this arena. Prophecy, genealogy, legal text and love letters are all potential candidates as well. What is the common ground here? Where is the interface with the Divine – that is, the eternal?

It is my conclusion that 'the Word of God' is our description of one interface between God in eternity and the time-matter universe which we observe around us. The Bible calls our location 'Creation', and firmly states that Creation was made by the agency of 'the Word of God' or 'the Spirit of God'. Without burdening scripture with the duty to correspond with every cosmological theory, it seems to me to be clear that the mysteries of expansion, the Big Bang, entropy and various immutable physical constants can be rooted in the mystery of a Deity operating outside time and space, and this situation is described consistently throughout the Bible. God's interface with the universe in its creation, maintenance and eventual end is pictorially described as by means of a 'Word'. What other way is there to describe such an incomprehensible relationship? A word is symbolic – linking one state to another. A word is transmissible. A word contains information which, like energy, as we know from physics, is conserved and cannot be lost.

Because God operates outside time, the Word issuing from him has an extra-temporal dimension to it; in other words, God's words continue to be spoken while we hear them, and before, and after. God, so to speak, started a conversation at Creation which continues all through history. Even the opening phrase of God's Word at Creation continues to resonate with unfinished business!

This is why prayer, wherein we mix our words with God's, is so tricky to understand. We are taking part in an eternal operation. Causality may not be respected (this should be a warning on the front of every prayer book!) We are results of God's Word – insofar as we are part of Creation. God uttered us when we became distinct from our mothers. In that sense, we also have an eternal origin and destiny. We return, conceptually, to the eternal structure that I have described at the beginning of these essays.

It seems clear that for the bare manuscripts to represent divine revelation, they must be read by people. The interaction between the words read and the reader's mind might form the junction, or interface, through which the word acts. It will be very hard to analyse this divine-human interface, and I suspect that to look too closely at the neuro-linguistic interface will result in the destruction of the interaction one is looking at! The process is complex and the many variables make it unlikely that any two people reading the same passage will understand exactly the same thing. Differences of language, usage, translation, personal character and situation will all have their effect (and this is only looking at some of the physical and human variables). When we add divine aspects to the mix, we can see that there is plenty of room for the Word to speak originally and relevantly into any situation. There is uncertainty in the action of any passage on any person who reads it. This uncertainty is limited by the overall meaning of the passage read – there is no license to twist a passage into any meaning one chooses. In fact, quite the opposite may be true. It might be better to say that as a person reads scripture, they themselves are 'read by' the divine writer. A passage elicits a reaction, and quite often this reaction tells us more about ourselves than we realise. Many readers of scripture have testified to the need to assimilate, or imbibe scripture – a process taking time, and akin to meditation. It is likely that this process is one of the ways in which the eternal Deity 'moors up' to our temporal minds.

A consequence of the eternal aspect to God's Word is that any action of Deity 'continues'. By this I mean that God's Creation is marked by persistence (and in this context, it is good to try to remove the sense of persistence 'over time' from the Word; we are trying to describe a persistence of 'being'). 'Uncreation', or the taking back of a word by God, is as hard to imagine as us 'unsaying' some misjudged comment. There may be in some part of God's providence 'uncreation', but I do not think that we can imagine such a thing, as it would be as if something which did exist had never existed at all. The concept of something 'never having existed' is mentioned in scripture in the book of Job, but only as an unfulfilled and desperate wish. To me, 'uncreation' stays in the realm of 'a concept which may or may not be impossible, which is not part of any plan that God has revealed, which we cannot imagine happening – but which we cannot exclude'. It seems to me that for now we have to assume the persistence of any part of God's Word – thus ourselves.

Another consequence of eternal speech would seem to be an element of incompleteness in any of God's words. This incompleteness is not because God is not a completer-finisher, but is related to our own human situation: we ourselves are not complete; time and space are still 'running'. We cannot therefore conceive of the 'completed Word'. The completed Word is something that is seen in eternity – that is, beyond time. Time may be part of it, but it is not limited to time. We can conceive of God's Word, but we cannot encompass it; therefore, we cannot really put it through the system of analytical criticism which we have applied to the books of the Bible.

Again, assimilation of scripture is a process that may take time; it is much more than the initial reaction on reading; it may be an ongoing conversation (perhaps over a lifetime for some passages!) which ends up with the same passage on paper and a radically altered reader. The books of the Bible are indeed part of the Word, but in saying that, we have to admit that their existence is greater than 'the words on the page'. This is not a particularly shocking revelation, as we commonly experience a verse from the Bible moving us to certain ideas and thoughts at one time, and then find that the same passage produces a different result in us at a different time. This is similar to the idea of a hologram, which reflects patterns from the same substance in different ways depending on the direction of light shone on it.

Simplistic critical approaches to scripture often fail to look at the portion of the Loch Ness monster 'under the water'. The part we see might be the simple translated meaning of the words. The part under the surface will be every personal reaction and effect that the reader undergoes – consciously or unconsciously – after reading the passage. It might include effects many years later, or, indeed, reflected words spoken to other people. Take the example of the historicity of Jonah; the story taken as a fable contains as much meaning as the story taken as historical narration. The point of recording it and including it in the Bible is not lost whichever way the historicity is seen. Whether it is 'literal' or not takes a secondary place to the moral of the tale. The question of literality for this book (and actually for all books, all testimony and everything said by anyone to anyone else in all of history) is incomplete.

Put another way, 'truth' is eternal. We are progressing along a timeline, thus for us 'truth' is an evolving entity. The nut and the kernel of the nut are, at present, one. We do not have a nutcracker – thus there are some possibilities which we cannot separate. We have to take all aspects of Jonah (and his big fish) together, and not try to separate them. Even the philosophic attempts to separate them into realities of concept, story, fact and science do not bring us to completion. Completion comes 'after' time has ceased to move. Whether this occurs after the ultimate heat death of the universe, or when the heavens are rolled up like a scroll, or, indeed, when we breathe our final breaths, is a question of perspective – I think!

To say that truth is evolving does not, however, mean that scripture cannot be definite or specific. Scripture is consistent in the things it says to the reader, despite the eternally unfolding nature of the Word, and the individual reactions we might have to the Word. It is as if we are sailing in a small boat over the vast oceanic swells of the creative power of God in history. We may not be able to see beyond the immediate waves which tower above our mast. We are forced to interact within the time and place we find ourselves – the present, and here – but we still sail in the direction that God takes us, we follow the course that he sets out clearly for us. That course is a composite of reading the Bible, inspiration from the inward voice, circumstances that we find ourselves in and the loving relationships within the Church of the saints. All these things are aspects of the Word to us, and we have the privilege of being the focus 'at this time and in this place' of God's creative nature. We wind the thread of our free will into the cloth, and it is 'our thread', uniquely from us. We do not see the completed pattern, but we do feel the way the weave is going – we feel the direction of the heave and roll of the mighty waters that we navigate. The scriptures in this context do not lose their power – to me they gain power, including in terms of literality, but also beyond that. When we come across a passage of scripture that challenges us, the correct, and sometimes difficult, course is to accept it and allow it to change us. If God has any power at all in scripture, it will be shown in the sparks that fly from our flint being struck by the Word of God assimilated. This course of action will certainly not end up with literal slavishness to dry words, but it also cannot ignore the thrust of emotion and intellect found coursing so strongly through the texts!

We now come back to the question I asked at the beginning of this chapter: When is a command not a command?

It is clear that when the Bible states something as a command – for example, one of the Ten Commandments – it is quite difficult to ignore, evolving truth or not. At the other extreme, some scriptural passages are recorded in such a way that it is evident they have specific intent for specific situations. For these passages, the process of cultural contextualisation may allow a better application of the language of scripture into the eternal intent of Deity. Nevertheless, we must allow scripture to speak to us even if the message does not correspond with our comfort zones! It would seem to me that those parts of scripture dealing with human relationships, especially those which remain consistent throughout the whole of the writing of the Bible, need to be taken as more directive than those which are more obviously political and organisational. The key must be always to approach scripture as one interface with Deity, never to be used slavishly, but always to be assimilated over a time, and brought into our prayer. The results, I believe, will be an eternal perspective and alignment of our developing being into the person we are always becoming.

CHAPTER ELEVEN

Uncertainty about God

Can God choose? If God is eternally good, and the ideal of all goodness, can he choose not to be that thing? Is there any freedom of action for God, as there must logically be only one 'best good' in any situation, which must be the choice God makes? Can God choose not to use the 'best good', but take another course of action? Is there a background good against which God himself must be judged; and if so, by whom?

These questions are examples of the many paradoxes which we inevitably encounter when considering the God who is all-loving, all-powerful and eternal. My basic answer to them all is summarised in stating that we are not limitless, and we can only imagine things related to our own context of time-passage. God, existing outside these limits, must confound us if we have the temerity to attempt to encompass him!

We must therefore accept uncertainty about God; and this begins with the most obvious aspect of God: we do not sense him directly! Of course, this is the major selling point for atheism, and also deism (which holds that there is a being who originates rationality and creation, but he is not directly knowable and is hidden from us). It is probable that God's intangibility is intrinsic to our position in his Creation, especially in relation to our time-bound nature. We are unfolding, thus our perception of the universe around us is also unfolding. We can only possibly appreciate God's deity within the context of the passage of time, which he created in its entirety. But he cannot be understood within that dimension, as he is illimitable in this respect.

Theological discussions regarding God disagree on almost every aspect of him that can be imagined, but it is traditional to believe that God created the universe ex nihilo – that is 'from scratch'. He was not limited by any presuppositions when he created. There was no rulebook before he created. On this issue, we can only conceive one limitation to God: himself! What limits that would impose on the sort of universe that God might possibly create can only be expressed in tautology, hopeless statements like, "God created what he would have created!" I think we can be content not to attempt to imagine it, but simply to accept that God created something consistent with his own nature. To state it negatively, God did not create something that opposes his own nature but something that was, nevertheless, distinct.

To use the human metaphor of decision-making, God 'chose' the nature of the universe he created. We must however eliminate two things from this choice: time and space! When we conceive of Creation being made by God, we automatically assume a time before and after; we also insert an arena of action. We cannot help it; like an optical illusion, our brain 'auto-corrects in' a film set around the Creation. This film set must be removed – as if we were using bluescreen techniques to remove all the surroundings from the action. Of course, to do this we have taken a negative action, and this raises other problems for our minds to grapple with.

As an example, when I remove time and space from my mental conception of God creating the universe, I end up with God being everything, subdividing a part of himself into a separate portion called, from that time on, 'Creation'. Is this an argument for God being Gaia? Is God the background out of which everything arose? Pantheism beckons! This conclusion might be the consequence if I did not understand that I had to negatively 'retouch' the image of Creation that my mind generated. Visualisation and verbalisation are the tools available and, unfortunately, they are not completely the right tools!

We must be content with statements of what we understand, which we shine upwards like searchlights. Occasionally, a flash of vision reveals a plane where two beams cross, but then the vision is lost, and the beams continue probing.

These are my searchlights:

a) God existed and exists and will exist – and is eternally not determined by any surroundings, or beholden to any prior cause or subsequent event.

b) It may be that God eternally causes his own context of action – but this must be an eternal context like himself and one not limited by three- or four-dimensional existence; it may be that these are the heavens; it may be that the Trinity – Father, Son and Holy Spirit – lives and works and eternally enjoys itself in a context, but we cannot describe it or imagine its edges or planes or geometry!

c) When God created the universe which we inhabit, this Creation was itself an event in an eternal context; it was a joyful expression of the art of the Trinity which made something that could be in relation to an eternal God, containing all of time and matter and space – itself the container, but distinct from God. The universe created had inside it cause and effect, temporal unfolding, spatial separation and particular interaction – in other words, all of the laws of nature that we discover. These laws work according to the eternal creative intent of God – in one sense they continue to be created, as to God the whole thing from beginning to end is 'within' his house.

d) Creation contains choices, logic, reason, causality and morality, and these are local to Creation – having meaning appropriate to their own context. Outside Creation we cannot know what they mean, even though it is clear that reason and morality at least have an eternal aspect. In this we are remarkably near to a deist position of ignorance of things we cannot prove. In contrast to the atheist's position, having an external God allows us to state that when logic and choice and causality cease, there is something else, and that is something which is also determined by the God who created the universe, and thus must also be consistent with God's eternal being.

e) To apply the concept of choice to God's actions can only be a gesture on our part to try to relate his actions to our own so that we can appreciate them. To expect that God should be bound by the rules of choice, as we are bound, is as wrong as to assume that when we make a sign, that actually is the thing signified rather than a symbolic act of representation.

f) God's context must proceed from himself, and that context is moral – in the sense that love is morality, and love is God's characteristic beyond any other description we can make of him. This morality is the source and foundation of all morals within our space and time.

All we have is our own universe, solar system, species and our cultures throughout history to judge by. We must be content with that, while admitting that God may not be limited by the same things as we are.

CHAPTER TWELVE

Uncertainty in Morals

Customs in the church and what a sin is.

What is the Church? From a human perspective, the Christian church represents the credal group who agree that they believe in the resurrection of Jesus Christ. We also believe in an eternal God and a revelation from him for everyone. The Creeds also state the commonality of believers across as many areas of human experience as possible and as clearly as possible; they include the doctrines of sin, the Trinity, Redemption and others. Lastly, the Christian churches have always attached importance to scripture as the major written source of revelation from God. Different traditions vary in their views of the fallibility and interpretation of the Bible, but every church calling itself Christian will consider scripture to have intrinsic authority, beyond the wisdom of people in the church in that generation.

Who is to say what the church is from the Divine perspective? What must it be like to perceive the work of recreation of humanity progressing through history and into the future mapped out, as if it were as one completed conjoining act between God and man? Might it be as if the whole of the history of the Church was compressed into the birth process of a new child?

God's interactions with humans as recorded in scripture have an essential morality. It is possible that this morality only applies to this space and time. It is possible that in eternity a different set of rules applies, but this does not seem likely, as every aspect of our world reflects in some degree its Creator. If morality is a reflection of a greater quality in God, then in some way it is essential to view morality as eternal. Let us therefore look at morality from an eternal perspective.

To view anything from the eternal perspective is alien to us. We can only sketch the eternal in similes. To do this we use tools including our memory, tradition, custom, records and teaching. We are equipped by our nature with a sticky memory, a rapid development of habits, a desire for conformity, sociability and an instinctive caution in behaviour. These tools extend from our immediate experience to apply to our whole lives, and on into our children's lives; in fact, to become traditions and cultures. We learn moral behaviours so efficiently that it is easy to see them, mistakenly, as innate (part of our nature) when they are much more frequently learned (part of our nurture). When we have learned these behaviours, we possess an inner voice that is so forceful that it almost appears audible. These tools derive from our mammalian heritage, and mark us out as the most successful species on our planet. They are our natural treasure, and we cling to them, for they have served us well. When we are faced by an unknown quantity, we bravely deploy them. We share them as communities jointly forming a perspective on a new challenge.

It is impossible to comprehend God, and in particular his morality, except to say, "He is good!" Nevertheless, we pragmatically take each fact and experience, and make it part of our human picture, using simile, parable and combinations of well-used words to describe the indescribable. We hand down these thoughts in traditions and they form part of our cultures – indeed, they form our truths.

When looking at the interface between the eternal God and mortal men, I am reminded of Peter at the Transfiguration. When confronted by Jesus meeting Elijah and Moses, Peter was unable to contribute anything very sensible to the glorious assembly. Instead, he fell back on offering to build some nice booths to somehow house the great event. The story does not comment particularly on this reaction of Peter's, and we are inclined to be a little embarrassed by it. On reflection, however, this might be simply an indication of the relationship between our own morality and heavenly morality. Our own traditions and cultures get built to 'house' eternal truths as expressed in the law and the prophets.

Building on this thought, it may be that scripture itself was recorded by people who were trying to put into words things which are outside our capability of describing or explaining. They used many of the tools that are noted above: parable, simile and tradition.

Some would include the scientific method and the rational search for truth as one of the most powerful combinations of these tools, honed into an industry of human activity which seeks to understand everything that we can understand.

I will restate my conviction that morality is an eternal feature which lights up our space-time universe from outside. I contend that morality comes from the eternal economy where Deity enjoys all things. In this view, morality is bound up in the very threads of the cloth of Creation. I would rapidly also state that morality in this sense is 'rightness', and can be applied as much to an earthquake as a relationship. There is, therefore, an application of morality to each level of Creation. Like the sciences, each level of Creation will possess its own 'moral language'. When we look at the inanimate world, whether galactic or quantum, that speech is in the language of physics and chemistry. When we look at humanity, that language is the language of society and of the Church. At each level, there is an expression of the eternal, appropriate to that level.

I will finish this treatment of the bridge between heavenly and earthly morality by taking four of its aspects within time and space: human nature, nurture and free will in a fallen world; the eternal expression of love as the source of morals to all of Creation after the fall; the Credo; and customs of the Church.

Human nature and a fallen world

It is Christian dogma that our world is fallen, fallen as a result of a human decision, interdependently fallen across all of Creation – nature and humanity.

I must redescribe the Fall within the eternal structure which I have outlined in previous chapters. The Fall was primarily an insult to love. The insult continues – as it contends with love which is an eternal characteristic of Creation. As already noted, Creation is an eternally spoken Word which has not ended at the present time (as the whole of time is part of – within – the creative thrust). That Word was, is and will be a Word of love. The Fall represents a reaction against love and is a continuing reaction at all points, and lasts as long as the Word of Creation does. The Genesis account of the Fall places it in the guise of a single decision by one man at one time. I will not 'open the container' which tells more about the historicity of the story of the eating of the apple of knowledge; indeed, I do not need to. The story itself (without a discussion of whether it 'actually occurred') tells enough of that eternal gluttony to show the relevance and power of that decision to influence all acts of all men, indeed to determine man's nature throughout our time and space. Genesis is clear that the single act of rebellion described has further consequences for the whole life of Adam. We might say that those consequences occur before, during and after the apple is bitten!

I have described in a previous chapter[15] some of the effects of the Fall on man. In another chapter[16], I looked at the Reformed doctrine of Total Depravity, picturing it as a warping out of shape of the nature of a man. The nature of a man runs throughout his life, and without intervention from God is misshapen, unable (as the doctrine of Total Depravity states) to produce a good result. We are dealing with a problem of the structure of every person, and that problem is not limited by our birth and death. The warped nature does not allow even the best-intended actions we make to hang in an acceptable pattern. We cannot connect with our eternal life until that warp is bent back into its proper shape as God intends. I use the word 'intends' as a description of God's desire within the Calvinist idea of his Unconditional Election: that is, the intent of the omnipotent being which must necessarily occur. In my belief, it is essential to assume that God's intent applies to every person in humanity. This is because we sit within the confines of space and time. We cannot guess or second-guess God's actual choice, except to always state that his choice is made as the perfect demonstration of love. This both Reformed and Arminian theology can depend on!

In previous chapters I have described a picture of the warp and weft of nature and nurture, shot through with threads of free will as if they were the coloured pattern which we individually produce in our lives.

---

[15] Chapter 2: What is the Fall of Man?
[16] Chapter 5: Destiny.

The Fall twisted our nature but this is only one part of the picture. It is important to notice that the effect of the Fall on Creation and humanity has twisted our nurture. What we experience from outside ourselves has at least an equal effect on our resultant structure. These two together are the framework on which we weave our own decisions. It is my belief, however, that with respect to morality, our free will is more significant than our nurture and nature. From an eternal perspective, the free-will decisions we weave into our lives form a pattern which defines our true self – which is an eternal definition. This pattern, which we weave from birth to death, cannot produce a good result unless the threads of our nature, warped out of shape, become 're-warped' by a conscious decision to relate to Christ. This decision is stated in the New Testament to be the decision to believe that Christ rose from death and became alive again. That decision is the nearest we can come to taking our Redemption out of eternity and looking at it as a single decision within time. Having said that, the natural place for the decision to believe is within the framework of our completed – that is, eternal – life. We can see it more easily if we pull back the camera to an eternal perspective and view ourselves as a completed whole. This necessarily introduces contradictions in our 'biographical story'! We see parts of our lives subsequent to our conversion as imperfect, and parts before conversion as better. My contention is that these views are only partial – "through a glass, darkly"[17] – and will be explained in the fullness of time.

Our nature within a fallen world is in the process of birth, and the fullness of time is simply the full term of our heavenly gestation.

The expression of love in morality

The Fall is an attack on Creation, thus as Creation is an unfolding event throughout the whole of time and space, so the Fall introduces an eternal twist into that Creation. In the same manner, and applying just as widely as the Fall, the redemptive love expressed in the incarnation of Jesus is an eternal splint that meets and cures each point of the twist of the Fall, so as to redeem Creation, and human nature where it

---

[17] 1 Corinthians 13:12 (KJV).

allows. This supportive reformation of Creation has occurred, is occurring and will occur.

Someone may ask, "If Redemption occurred contiguously with the Fall and with Creation, how then can we distinguish them – is the end result not going to be simply 'a new creation', without the tedious need to untwist Creation-Fall-Redemption?" This is a good question, and one that I cannot answer adequately! Will we, from within eternity – after we have risen to meet Jesus – look back (or down?) on our lives, and see a simple untarnished, untwisted whole from our birth to our death? Will we be able to distinguish unredeemed from redeemed in ourselves?

My inadequate answer is that God chose to do it this way, and who am I to question God? Gracious – I sound like Job! The smallest Brownian vibration of a heavenly quark will be ample to disrupt the totality of hell's assault on God's joyful effervescence of the Creation-Fall-Redemption story. Will 'this life' have been significant? Well, the part of us which gives us our individuality (our free will) seems to arise from within the space-time confines of our lives, and has its own mystery. I suspect that this is very significant, despite being small in the context of heaven. Perhaps this alone is a reason why God decided the whole 'experiment' of this universe was worth it?

The fact that God does seem to think this Creation is a worthwhile exercise reaffirms the view that morality is the expression of love. That is, morality *is* love. Morality is rightness, which is goodness, which is love. I said that redemptive love turns to meet every twist in fallen Creation. I also implied that this love is applied at different levels of Creation. Is there morality in an earthquake? Is there in a water snail? Can a chimpanzee be bad? It is clear that our theology must be applied appropriately to the level we are dealing with. This view of morality implies that each level of Creation that we can perceive (or even understand, with no possibility of perception) has been affected by the Fall. It also implies that each level of Creation is also being redeemed by the application of love. Of course, when applying love to an earthquake, we must not change the earthquake into something it is not (sentient!) but love enables us to see the earthquake in its rightful place. We apply this at each level of Creation, guided by science, using language appropriate to the level we deal with. We know that each science has its own phenomenology, and this is derived *post hoc.* For example, we do not predefine the nature of a water snail; we observe it, and we let it tell us how to deal with it. There is a link to the nominative power of Adam here; perhaps we have been given authority to name all things. This 'naming' is shorthand for the processes of perception, observation, experience and eventually reflection. We then express them back to the Creator who enjoys our description.

My contention is that just as man can name each part of Creation that he can perceive, each part of Creation has also been twisted out of shape by man's Fall. This 'power to name', corrupted by the Fall, results in a failed relationship between man and Creation at every level. The good news is that redemptive love meets every twist, and defines a morality which is applicable to everything that we can name. In summary, all things we know about have a sort of morality, and love applies to every level of Creation.

Creeds are linked to God's redemptive love

There are, therefore, necessary implications for our current behaviour within the Creeds.

In opposition to any moral behaviour is the observation that 'nature' does not simply tell us what is right or wrong. Variations of species, culture and individual inclination seem to generally support a pragmatic sociological attitude to morals. We see this in full swing in our own enlightened culture.

Nevertheless, I hope I have illustrated in previous chapters that Creation is an outpouring of God's love, and is surrounded by an eternal environment which is completely attuned to 'loving God'. We are creatures within Creation, but we are 'under construction'. When we are completed, we will find ourselves within that eternal environment. That destiny means that we must and will develop into creatures that correspond to the environment which we will inhabit eternally. That environment is one of love; that is, 'divine morality'.

I therefore conclude that morality has an independent reality, external to our time and space and it is relevant now – despite appearances!

We see the consequences of the Fall all around us, and generally they can be summarised as attacks on love, or as disconnections with nature because of the effects of these attacks. Death is the termination of our timeline within Creation, and it seems that death is linked with attacks on love. "The sting of death is sin," says 1 Corinthians 15:56. We therefore come back to morality – love – as the lost connection between us and a satisfactory existence.

We codify our belief as a Church in verbal expressions of those things that have been found to be true. There is an element of faith in these expressions, but we take what we have and earnestly refine it to match what we have experienced, what we have been told and what wells up in our hearts when we react to these wonderful things. We recite these searchlight statements as Creeds, which so miserably fail to describe the grandeur of God; but in doing so, we align ourselves with the redemptive purpose of God, and rehearse the morals (the love) which we believe are growing in us. Thus, our actual behaviour must come to reflect our Creeds. We will be and become the good person we have described in our words. Our word must sub-create our future selves in an echo of God's creative-redemptive Word which initiated and completes the incarnation of Jesus.

In the last few decades there has been a trend to try to 'find oneself', as if our nature (the part of us which is there to be found) was the only part of ourselves worth finding. I hope in this chapter to have at least opened up the possibility that our nature is only one aspect of our selves. At least as important is our nurture – and probably these two put together fail to reach half the importance of our own free will. To put it another way, we 'find ourselves' by exercising that free will. Those actions of free will exert a tension on our nature and our nurture. The result will be a failure without the re-warping that comes from a decision to believe in Christ and his resurrection.

When we say the Creed, and when we enact it in our lives, we are, in effect, freely choosing to mould ourselves into the image of love. It is important to both say and do something – both speech and action are dimensions of free will.

In this more complex structure, I would suggest that the parts of our nature that goad us and drag us into unloving behaviour can be seen as things that in God's eternal economy will take rather different positions of importance. Sometimes the Bible seems irritatingly out of touch with our society (for example when sexual behaviour is examined). Nevertheless, if we patiently let scripture work its way through us, my experience is that it has a better grasp of the ways in which we can align with eternal love than we have. My conviction is that in the exercise of our free will – especially by saying and doing the things we are taught by scripture – we allow eternal love to mould our eternal structure into our 'true self'.

The customs and traditions of the church

"Do church traditions and customs represent morality?" This is a question that has produced many opinions!

My touchstone is love, when answering specific questions about behaviour, and thus we need to consider what is right or wrong, what is advisable or inadvisable, so that we can act lovingly. It seems that every scriptural culture has codified a moral legislature, and there are cogent themes to those rulebooks found throughout the Bible. All the rulebooks come under the heading of "Love God" or "Love thy neighbour", but there are definite cultural elements found when all the rulebooks are analysed. Dress codes and the rules about roles of men and women in society may indeed change with cultures, as these deal with relatively superficial matters when it comes to 'loving as God loves'. We cannot escape completely from rules affecting our sexual behaviour, though; it is clear from looking at the whole of scripture that God created the human body and mind (biologically and psychologically) in a specific form. Science does not enlighten us as to the best morals, but it seems to me that scripture consistently holds us to a set of behaviours which cannot be derived from a purely biologically or psychologically argued position. In other words, scripture has its own viewpoint!

I therefore argue that it is perfectly normal for a church to have its own culture, mores and customs, provided these do not contradict scripture as noted below. They must be adhered to voluntarily, not imposed by social pressure or diktat. They must result in an increase in love throughout the body.

Separate from, but often congruent with, these customs are the rulebooks we find in scripture. There is some cultural interpretation and modification seen within scripture itself, especially as the New Testament develops, which guides us into a reasonable flexibility when it comes to condensing all the rulebooks in scripture into codes of conduct for modern people to use. Some parts of the Levitical law have obvious relevance to our society today; others are clearly designed for the culture of the time. There is always the possibility of doubt when it comes to the commandments of the Bible, and this doubt should lead us to examine and re-examine the commands written so long ago, to reach a practical balance, just as Paul did for the Corinthian church. When we have gone through this process and find that the commands are repeated consistently throughout scripture, I think that no amount of cultural change in our society can justify jettisoning these rules. My logic is that, on a purely human level, scripture was written over a time period that exceeds, by several times over, the total length of time that our particular culture has lasted. That "there is nothing new under the sun"[18] is still true, even when we consider genetic engineering, feminism, political creeds and interplanetary travel!

---

[18] Ecclesiastes 1:9.

CHAPTER THIRTEEN

Uncertainty about Love

What is love? Can it be defined except by itself? How do we measure the length of a tape measure? Do we use another tape measure, or can we find something else?

We tend to assume that we know what love is, but we frequently disagree about how it should actually work. The famous 1 Corinthians 13 passage defines love in thirteen memorable verses (surely the best cure for superstition about that number!) Some verses say what love is, some what it is not; most relate to actions or other qualities (patient, kind, not selfish) which mark a deed or a person as aligned with love. Nevertheless, we still find it hard to say exactly what would be the most loving thing to do.

As an example, when our child asks to watch TV, what should we do to love them? It might be best for them not to watch; but what if the child is then sad? Should I let the child watch, risking that they be exposed to material that could harm them? Complex decisions arise when asked the simplest of questions. These relate to the uncertainty we have and our lack of knowledge (especially about what the truth is about another person!) Time and distance are, as always, adversaries, preventing our having a complete knowledge of what would be 'the best for them'. It is clear that the perspective of an eternal existence would give a much more reliable view from which to judge what is loving and what is not. Like someone with a broken tumble dryer, I hope to suspend my answers to these uncertainties between two supports. The supports are these: that love is eternal; and that love is a matter of choice.

Firstly, my contention is that love is primarily an eternal relationship or an eternal language (if that is any clearer). An act of love does not stand by itself in one place at one time; to be a loving act, it is connected to every other loving act, from the beginning to the end of time. It is, in fact, connected to God! This may seem a slightly odd way to look at love, but if we move on to the second support mentioned above, I hope it will become clear why there is a timeless aspect to love which is essential to our understanding of it.

My second support is that in our space-time universe, in everything we experience or know, love is a matter of choice. It is subject to free will. There is the possibility of love and of 'not love'. In some sense, every chance to express love is balanced by a chance not to. Is there any love if there is not a choice? If we loved without choice, then that would seem to us to be 'less like love'! Without sacrifice it is hard to conceive love.

This aspect of love begs the question, "In heaven, is God faced with a choice to love or 'not love' in all his acts?" I am now at the limit of my grasp, for the question seems too hard to me! This difficulty is more with the nature of choice than with the nature of love, however. We accept that free will is the exercising of choice by a person, in this context determining whether to love or not to love. Is free will, then, a specific characteristic of our time and space? Are things indeterminate only as looked at from one spot and at one instant? Calvinist doctrine would seem to imply that if you 'go eternal', things become fixed (predestined). In eternity there is, so to speak, only love when we get right down to it. This conclusion brings us back to the eternal nature of love. It seems that we cannot really understand love without being 'eternal'.

Conversely, we see that in time and space, uncertainty is always going to be a characteristic of love.

My first example of this is related to the other person (the love object). When we love, we act, and hope that the person we love will receive what we have sent! Sometimes it is almost certain that we have acted lovingly; at other times we find that we did not manage to get it right. This existential problem in relationships does not invalidate our attempts to live in love. What is the very best for a person? Sometimes nobody knows, including the person themselves! We still act lovingly, but there is no certainty. We have to exercise belief before we can do any good.

My second example relates to us. When we act lovingly, are we doing it for the other or for ourselves? It is surprisingly difficult to find a truly disinterested love. Doubt as to our own motives must be admitted and worked through; often a period of many years is needed to get to know what acts constitute 'genuine love' for us.

The solution to uncertainty is primarily to exercise our faith. This dynamic must form the backdrop to our whole life as a developing eternal being. We must act, not in certainty, but using every piece of knowledge and experience we possess, and when this fails us, taking a leap into the unknown. We must continually learn and relearn, honing our habits into the shape that fits the being we are becoming. In this context, love is a process of the school of life. We do not do this because we are told to; we do it because we find that we are becoming 'a lover'. The length of our days is hardly enough to start the change! We are also changing ourselves to match a change within. I spoke in Chapter 5 about a re-warping of our nature. If Redemption means anything, it means that we have fundamentally changed our internal landscape so that anything unloving brings us discomfort, like a stone in your shoe. It becomes more and more important to attend to these discomforts, because they are aids to making us ready to live in an eternal love.

We were told by Augustine to "love, and do what you like"[19]. Although this promises to make everything simpler, as we said above, it is frequently difficult to know what the loving thing is for a particular moment. This uncertainty as to whether we are indeed loving means that the complexities of behaviour remain as difficult as ever.

To solve this problem, it is more helpful to see love as more than an act. If we see that love is a state of being as well as a doing, things become simpler. Augustine's motto becomes, "If you are a lover, you can rely on your instincts to guide you into the correct actions."

The question then arises, "How can I 'be love'?"

---

[19] Augustine of Hippo (354-430). *A sermon on love.*

You cannot lift yourself up by your shoelaces, and you cannot will yourself into being a lover. To be transformed into a state of love may be more like catching an infection than an exercise in willpower. It might be that we 'catch it' when we are susceptible to it.

I can only tell you how to be in the right place at the right time to catch the love infection; I cannot tell you how to change your nature, although it is a change of nature that we need.

I referred to the change of nature in Chapter 1. It is completely essential to the state of love we wish to enter. The change takes place when we decide to believe in the resurrection of Jesus Christ who was crucified. The daily decision to accept that reality is the lever that slots us into the right place to be love. If you like musical analogies, the act of belief pulls the strings of our life into the correct tension to be played in tune. I do not think there is much more to it than that, from a human point of view, although the daily decision to believe should include actions that reinforce that decision. It is interesting that after we believe, we often seem to form our own curriculum of study and exercise through simply following the thoughts and desires which we experience in the wake of the 'belief'. I cannot guide you through those things; they are unique to you. It is a source of wonder to me that these reactions in us following a step of belief seem to demonstrate that the eternal God acts specifically and harmonically in response to every one of us. This is the joy of faith!

When we have embarked on our daily step of belief, we will note changes in our preferences and comfort zones. These are the marks of us becoming lovers. While not totally automatic, and always requiring an act of will, these new preferences reflect a change in our nature. Part of the Christian life is to be aware of, understand and reflect on these fruits. These are the "fruit of the Spirit"[20]. All the fruit of the Spirit can be summarised as 'the habits of the lover'.

---

[20] Galatians 5:22.

Chapter Fourteen

The Fear of Death

If we are asked what is the ultimate emotion that we experience, we might be torn between desire and fear. If I am honest in my self-assessment, the motivation for much of my thought and daily concern is a balance. On one side, there is the desire for fulfilment, pleasure and self-expression. On the other side, there is the fear of loss, shame and pain. It seems quite clear that humans weave the cloth of their lives in a way that expresses their day-to-day tack between these two great flows. They are both intimately linked to uncertainty.

Psychologists have built up an impressive structure describing the human mental map. This discipline tries to help therapists and scientists understand how we function. I must defer to them in their explanations for many of our personality traits and behavioural rules. Nevertheless, I think that this exercise is ultimately limited to describing what we observe. As I said in the first chapter, if we limit our selfhood to a biological or psychological description, the features that make us 'ourselves' end up fading into a dreamlike notion with little substance.

To move on from a scientific or clinical description of ourselves to something that reflects our real conviction that we actually mean something requires a step further than simple scientific observation.

If you have read this far, you may be able to guess that, for me, this step is to link desire and fear to our eternal structure!

First, I would suggest that both desire and fear are natural expressions of any higher organism, and we see them in dogs, cats and animals of all sorts. They are brought to a peak of expression in humans, and especially in the creation of art.

Second, I would maintain that both are firmly seated in time, and vary throughout our lives. In this sense, I would separate them from our 'being', and say that they are not to be confused with our real selves. They are an outflow from us, but not our essential heart. This statement is easy to make, but I must admit that it is very hard to really understand; there is a large body of opinion which would state that we (our perceived selves) are no more than the expressed balance of our emotional reactions.

Third, desire and fear affect the way we express our free will. Those threads that build up our real self are often woven in as a result of a deep desire for fulfilment, or a deep fear of rejection. I will state that by themselves, desire and fear do not explain our free will. I believe that we can weave free choices into our lives which are not controlled by our desires and fears. This belief is hard to prove, but I will now try to show why I believe that our free will is more than simply a reaction to what we desire and what we fear!

It is my conviction (and I would ask you to check carefully if you agree with me here) that all desire is really a desire for life, and all fear is actually a fear of death. You may see apparent contradictions to this thesis in those who seem to desire death and those who fear life. I would maintain that in these people, the fear and the desire have been misplaced, by illness, trauma or other major influences. These influences are often found in our nurture, and are almost never seen as normal. I am not going to use this chapter to discuss the huge and important topics of suicide and self-harm, but would ask the reader to follow me, for the moment, if I repeat that in general, and normally, almost all our fears are summed up in the fear of death. Death in this sense is the ultimate loss, and the universal human expression of helplessness. Our desires, in this picture, are a reflection of the fears, and thus move us towards all the things that death deprives us of – pleasure, self-determination and well-being.

Fear thus shows us that there is one universal human language which everyone understands, from the Neanderthal in his cave to the aesthete in his penthouse. I dealt with it in Chapter 2, and we return to that point now. It is the Fall. Every one of us can identify with this story in some way. Thus, the solution to that tragedy continues to be Resurrection, and the relinking of our orphaned selves with our eternal being. When this occurs, we see fear and desire in their proper context. They are really the two guardian pillars either side of the door of our uncertainty. Because we live in this space-time universe, they loom large and we cannot open the door. All we can do is to use every scrap of knowledge and understanding we possess, and then take a final step of faith. This faith is to say that behind the opaque barrier of uncertainty, we believe that one man died but now lives. In this way, the belief in the Resurrection is the answer to the fundamental fear – thus to all fears. This belief also answers the uncertain and fleeting desires which presently motivate our decisions: "solid joys and lasting treasure, none but Zion's children know."[21]

---

[21] From the hymn 'Glorious things of thee are spoken' by John Newton; *Olney Hymns.*

CHAPTER FIFTEEN

A Short Final Note on Joy and Happiness

Much has been made of the differences between and similarities of joy and happiness. Both seem to be seen as positive states to be in, but the latter is often stated to be less substantial and more fleeting.

It seems to me that the work of the Spirit of God in causing the fruit of joy to spring from children of God gives a clue as to the nature of that blessing. A fruit growing from an eternal source would seem to be less dependent on time than a purely human emotion. Indeed, those who write about joy convey a sense of the timeless – a memory, or a recurring dream to which one returns in time of trouble.

Perhaps we should regard the welling up of joy in our hearts as the rising of a spring of water from a river that flows beneath the ground across which we walk for many miles (like MacDonald's hero in Lilith), hearing the sound of rushing water while surrounded by an arid land.

Maybe we can think of it as a deep thrumming harmony in the darkness that has a rhythm which catches our hearts into a beat that matches it; if so, the harmony is widespread over many moments in our lives, and cannot be caught without spreading our perception into a broader net than the simple momentary flight of happiness.

The image I want to convey is of harmony between our hearts and the music of heaven, an 'Ohrwurm' so much more desirable and wholesome, a song that takes us home, a scent on the wind that wrenches us out of our cares and causes us to be like Mole:

"...he stopped dead in his tracks, his nose searching hither and thither in its efforts to recapture the fine filament, the telegraphic current, that had so strongly moved him. A moment and he had caught it again; and with it this time the recollection in its fullest flood."[22]

For this joy is more like being reunited with your own self, a self from a good and desirable time, a self that is united with every good relationship and fortune that exists in your history. Indeed, in some ways this reuniting extends beyond our own memories and experience, for it includes the imagination and dreams long forgotten, brought into a synchrony and built into a substantiality that for a second or two unites us with the eternal.

It is this eternal dimension that I think distinguishes joy from pleasure and happiness. The latter are point gradients; the former is the integral of the curve. The latter indicate a trajectory, but the former a state of being. Did I say an eternal state? Hardly that in this vale of shadows; but surely our sharply focussed sense of self is widened and deepened by joy to perceive reality more clearly? Maybe we can start to grasp the holographic composite of more than just the time and place we happen to be in. Perhaps in these moments of joy we peer between the slats in the fence to see the real work on the new heavens and earth progressing in God's building site behind the hoardings!

---

[22] Kenneth Grahame; *The Wind in the Willows.*

APPENDIX

"...a discovery of something that we already were."

My brain catches fire, especially if I am not disturbed. It grows, I develop it more and more, ever more clearly. The work is then finished in my skull, or really just as if, even if it is a long piece, and I can embrace the whole in a single glance, as if it were a painting or a statue. In my imagination, I do not hear the work in its flow, as it must appear in succession, but I have the whole in one block, as it were. What a gift! Invention, elaboration, all that happens within me as in a magnificent, grandiose dream, but when I manage to super-hear the assembled totality, that's the best moment ... it is perhaps the greatest benefit for which I must thank the Creator.[23]

Mozart

For as a craftsman, taking beforehand in his mind the form of the thing to be made, carries out the effect of his work, and leads it through the orders of time what he had seen simply and in the mode of the present, so God arranges the things that are to be made singly and stably through providence, but he administers the very things he has arranged through fate in a multiple, temporal way.[24]

Boethius

---

[23] Cited by Jean and Brigitte Massin Massin, Jean & Brigitte (1970); Wolfgang. Amadeus Mozart. Paris: Fayard (p 474).

[24] Boethius, *Consolations;* 4.6.12.

Your machine, which uses cylinders, pulleys and corporeal materials, did not exist corporeally in your foreknowledge, but here imagination contained, in an incorporeal and living way, the logos of what was to be, whereas the machine came into being corporeally, put together out of inner knowledge which was not such. If this is how things are in your creation, what would you say of the foreknowledge of the gods, in which pre-exists what is, for us, is ineffable, truly indescribable and impossible to circumscribe ... the gods know divinely and intemporally what depends on us, and we act as we naturally tend to do, and what we choose is foreknown to them, not by the term in us, but to the one in them. [25]

Proclus

The nature of light

It is generally assumed that a radiating body emits light in every direction, quite regardless of whether there are near or distant objects which may ultimately absorb that light; in other words that it radiates "into space." This assumption has seemed natural and convenient. We know that on a clear night objects radiate energy into what seems empty space, but I am not aware that any exact experiments have been made at different altitudes to eliminate the effect of the atmosphere and to determine whether the emission is that which would be given by Steffan's law. In any case we do not know how much cold matter the universe may contain.

I am going to make the contrary assumption that an atom never emits light except to another atom, and to claim that it is as absurd to think of light emitted by one atom regardless of the existence of a receiving atom as it would be to think of an atom absorbing light without the existence of light to be absorbed. I propose to eliminate the idea of mere emission of light and substitute the idea of transmission, or a process of

---

[25] *Proclus On Providence; 12, 65.*

exchange of energy between two definite atoms or molecules. Now, if the process be regarded as a mere exchange, the law of entire equilibrium, which I have recently advanced, requires us to consider the process as a perfectly symmetrical one, so that we can no longer regard one atom as an active agent and the other as an accidental and passive recipient, but both atoms must play coordinate and symmetrical parts in the process of exchange.

I shall not attempt to conceal the conflict between these views and common sense. The light from a distant star is absorbed, let us say, by a molecule of chlorophyll which has recently been produced in a living plant. We say that the light from the star was on its way toward us a thousand years ago. What rapport can there be between the emitting source and this newly made molecule of chlorophyll? Suppose we make this same star the source of light in the apparatus of figure 1. By opening the second slit we prevent a particle of light from reaching the point C. Do we therefore prevent its original emission? If so it would mean that we could, perhaps in a trivial way, but nevertheless in principle, alter the course of past events.

Such an idea is repugnant to all of our notions of causality and temporal sequence; but we must remember that these notions have arisen from the observation of complex processes which are very different from the elementary reversible processes which we are here considering. Unless the result of some actual fact of experiment or observation can be brought against the new view we need not be deterred by this conflict with common notions. Indeed we shall see that there are already some inconsistencies between prevailing physical ideas and that geometry which so admirably interprets the kinematics of relativity.[26]

Gilbert. N. Lewis

---

[26] Gilbert. N. Lewis; PROC. N. A. S. PHYSICS VOL. 12, 1926.

The transactional interpretation of quantum mechanics and quantum nonlocality

We note here that the sequence of stages in the emitter-absorber transaction presented here employs the semantic device of "pseudo-time", describing a process between emitter and absorber extending across lightlike or timelike intervals of spacetime as if it occurred in a time sequence external to the process. This is only a pedagogical convention for the purposes of description. The process itself is atemporal, and the only observables come from the superposition of all of the steps that form the final transaction.[27]

John G. Cramer

The Einstein papers: a man of many parts

A human being is a part of the whole, called by us "Universe", a part limited in time and space. He experiences himself, his thoughts and feelings as something separated from the rest – a kind of optical illusion of his consciousness. This delusion is a kind of prison for us [...] our task must be to free ourselves from this prison [...].[28]

Einstein

Barker's revelation

"Nothing has ever happened," repeated Barker, with a morbid obstinacy.
"You don't know what a thing happening means? You sit in your office expecting customers, and customers come; you walk in the street expecting friends, and friends meet you; you want a drink, and get it; you feel inclined for a bet, and

---

[27] John G. Cramer; 28 Feb 2015; arXiv: 1503.00039 Cornell university library.
[28] W. Sullivan, New York Times, March 29, 1972. See Hadot 2011, 169; 205 n. 4.

make it. You expect either to win or lose, and you do either one or the other. But things happening!" and he shuddered ungovernably.

"Go on," said Buck, shortly. "Get on."

"As we walked wearily round the corners, something happened. When something happens, it happens first, and you see it afterwards. It happens of itself, and you have nothing to do with it. It proves a dreadful thing – that there are other things besides one's self. I can only put it in this way. We went round one turning, two turnings, three turnings, four turnings, five. Then I lifted myself slowly up from the gutter where I had been shot half senseless, and was beaten down again by living men crashing on top of me, and the world was full of roaring, and big men rolling about like nine-pins." [29]

---

[29] *The Napoleon of Notting Hill;* Book IV Chapter I
www.gutenberg.org/cache/epub/20058/pg20058.txt

Related Books by the Publisher

Free Will: God's Choice, Our Choice
A. E. Mitchell
ISBN 978-1-78815-659-2

Free Will: God's Choice, Our Choice considers the implications of God's decision to grant freedom of choice to all humankind, and seeks to address questions such as: What exactly is free will? Why did God grant humankind free will? If humankind has free will, who is in charge, God or humans?

Using both real life experiences and hypothetical scenarios, A. E. Mitchell offers helpful explanations backed up with Scripture, for those who have puzzled over the relationship between God and evil. These are helpful suggestions as to how Christians can understand God's responses to prayer, interpret the Bible, deal with concepts such as fairness, forgiveness and judgement, and address issues such as sex and war.

Exquisite Jesus
Keith Jackson
ISBN 978-1-911086-38-3

When we encounter Jesus, we find that his life is full of paradoxes. He is great yet vulnerable; human yet divine; born, but of a virgin; the Life, yet he died; without sin yet suffered divine punishment; ascended to Heaven yet always with us; followed by some but rejected by others.

In short, Jesus is exquisite: beautiful, lovely, superb, valuable, delicate, priceless, beyond description and more.

This book looks at these and other paradoxes and tries to unravel just who Jesus is and what His life means for us today. As you read through these pages, you will find yourself falling in love with Him again – or maybe even meet Him for the first time.